Taunton's
NEW
Front Yard
IDEA BOOK

SANDRA S. SORIA

The Taunton Press

The Taunton Press
Inspiration for hands-on living®

The Taunton Press, Inc.
63 South Main Street, PO Box 5506
Newtown, CT 06470-5506
e-mail: tp@taunton.com

Editor: Erica Sanders-Foege
Copy editor: Nina Rynd Whitnah
Indexer: Heidi Blough
Jacket/Cover design: Kimberly Adis
Interior design: Kimberly Adis
Layout: Laura Lind Design
Illustrators: Tinsley Morrison (pp. 128–129), Melissa Lucas (pp. 24–25), Martha Garstang (p. 31),
Steven Cominsky (p. 104)
Cover Photographer: Front cover: © Eric Roth; Back cover: (clockwise from top) © Mark Lohman,
© Mark Lohman, © Brian Vanden Brink, © Bruce Nyenhuis

Library of Congress Cataloging-in-Publication Data

Soria, Sandra S.
  Taunton's new front yard idea book / author: Sandra S. Soria.
      p. cm.
  ISBN 978-1-60085-371-5
  1. Landscape gardening. I. Title. II. Title: New front yard idea book.
  SB473.S63 2011
  635.9--dc23
                          2011031060

Printed in the United States of America
10 9 8 7 6 5 4 3 2

acknowledgments

I OFFER SPECIAL THANKS TO MY editor, Erica Sanders-Foege, for her guidance and humor throughout the twisting, turning process of getting a book to the presses. Thanks go out to photo editor Katy Binder as well, who knows just when to say, "Let me know what I can do to make this easier." And thanks to the talented editors and designers of *Fine Gardening* magazine for sharing their deep well of know-how with me.

To the photographers and landscape experts whose work you see within these covers, I owe a huge debt of gratitude. Their eyes and hands truly do make a prettier world.

And, last but never least, a loving thanks to my family. My husband, Rick, and our sons, Lucca and Elijah, not only know how to put up with the moods of a writer, but they also know how to put up with her messes.

contents

introduction

AN YOU IMAGINE MOVING INTO your home with just your basic furniture, living without art, accessories, or entertainment gear? It would be a dull and uninviting place...and you might not want to spend a lot of time in it.

If your front yard is appointed only with the basics—a front stoop and a bank of foundation plantings, say—you're also missing an opportunity to create an open-air living space that is comfortable, functional, and interesting. Envision your front yard with layers of colorful plant life, a small seating area just off the front entry, and a winding flagstone path. Not only are the hard angles of your house and yard softened, you and your family also have an excuse to go outside and play...or just relax and enjoy the neighborhood action.

Best of all, the front yard offers the opportunity for the do-it-yourselfer in all of us to get our hands dirty while extending the beauty and function of our homes. There are many landscaping projects to tackle that don't require expert-level skills. You'll find

information on these in the pages that follow. You'll also find inspiration for more extensive schemes and the advice you need to find the pros that can help you get the job done.

Boosting the curb appeal of your home has advantages beyond even improved aesthetics and family fun. If you're in the market to sell your house, a pulled-together front yard makes a "vital first impression," according to the real estate Appraisal Institute. In fact, real estate studies show that exterior projects consistently outperform interior improvements in return on investment, with many surveys indicating the return to be 120 percent. Not bad!

Whether you do it for the sale of your home or for yourself, if you put some of the hundreds of ideas in this book into play in your front yard, you'll see many paybacks, not the least of which is the pride and satisfaction of turning your home turf into a personal and welcoming oasis that greets you warmly each time your wheels turn into the driveway.

getting started

WHEN CONSIDERING ALL THE IMPROVEMENTS YOU CAN MAKE TO YOUR home, it makes a lot of sense to begin before you even get to the front door. The front yard is the face you present to the world. Why not give it all the attention you pay to the front room?

The benefits of a well-planned front yard actually go well beyond beauty. With the right planning, a front-yard design defines your property borders, reduces the need to heat or cool your home, saves on water costs, and can even help boost the value of your property.

To you and your family, the rewards of a well-thought-out landscape go beyond dollars and cents. Carve out a courtyard around the front door and you've extended your living space into the open air. Create a foliage-lined path to your entryway and you've extended a gracious greeting to friends and family. A lush lawn enclosed by a fence, garden, or hedge provides the kids a plush and protected place to play.

You can show off your personality and enhance the whole neighborhood with the right landscaping elements. In this historic neighborhood, color and creativity are welcome, but formal symmetry links the home with its neighbors.

Deciding what type of front-yard atmosphere is right for you should be guided by your climate, your home's architectural style and site, and your lifestyle. So, before you grab a shovel to dig in, do some planning. Picking up this book is a good first step. As you flip through the information and ideas that follow, think about your goals for your front yard. As with most projects, doing a little research first will—in the end—save you time, energy, and money.

assessing your architecture

● ● ● IT USED TO BE EASY TO DESIGN A FRONT yard. Lay down turf that stretches like wall-to-wall carpet from the street to the traditional lineup of shrubs that skirt the house. Keep the lawn manicured and the bushes trimmed for the neighborhood's sake, and save the fun and frivolity for the privacy of the backyard.

No more. Our neighbors are fearlessly planting perennial beds in full view and breaking up the buffer zone of evergreens with swaying grasses and blooming bushes. The benefit of adding pretty plantings and focal-point features is obvious: front yards not only deserve this attention, but they cry out for it. Cement drives and squared-off stoops demand softening, just as our boxy houses could use more warmth, color, and dimension.

When envisioning how to improve your front yard, consider the house itself. Think of a landscaping plan as an extension of your house rather than just a way to pretty up the place, and you're on your way to creating an environment that welcomes guests and enhances your home.

Without a few plants and curving paths, this chalet ranch house would be all straight lines and sharp angles. The progression of stone, flowers, and plant life creates a warmer welcome without obscuring the home's design.

These homeowners wanted a buffer from their busy street. A layering of trees, grasses, and boulders—both natural and manufactured—surrounding a new brick path creates an intriguing entrance for guests while it blocks sights and sounds.

architectural styles

● ● ● TAKING YOUR CUES FROM YOUR HOME'S design is a straightforward place to start your plan. After all, if you call a small cottage *home*, you wouldn't want to fight the inherent charm with sleek, modern landscape elements. Likewise, a modern home would lose its design edge surrounded by a picket fence and a tumble of colorful flowers.

Walk to the street or the bottom of the driveway and take a look at your house with a critical eye. Is it as warm and welcoming as you'd like it to be? Does your landscape feel like a part of the house? Would your home benefit from more color? Or could it use a bit of softening and layering? How can you ease the transition between outdoors and in? When you stand in the living room and look out, are the colors harmonious? These are some of the things to think about as your front-yard plan develops.

Suburban homes are breaking the traditional formula of a manicured turf plus a buffer of evergreens. Swaying grasses and blooming perennials soften the façade of this new house.

ABOVE This California cottage gets extra doses of charm thanks to colorful flower beds, a curving path, and a picket fence that adds definition to the tumble of vibrant blooms.

LEFT An ultramodern residence needs equally spare landscaping elements. Notice how sleek gray pavers echo the aluminum window trim, and the grassy courtyard mimics the square planes of the home itself.

This Midwestern ranch house is softly framed by multiple beds filled with grasses, evergreens, and subtly blooming sedums. Too much color would have detracted from the home's low-slung brick-and-stone exterior.

This classic Cape Cod house is loved for its symmetry. A center path and mirrored plantings on either side play up the formality while softening the starkness of the home.

The benefits of marrying the right landscape elements to architecture are readily apparent on the East Coast island of Nantucket. Purple hydrangeas and Russian sage are classic companions to the uniform, weathered-gray-shingled houses of the island.

ABOVE Desert homes offer obvious challenges to the home landscaper. That's why the owner of this modern Southwestern home opted to repeat a single type of plant but break up the monotony with large containers and a partial wall.

This contemporary farmhouse has an asymmetrical, or unbalanced, landscape plan. A wide and covered front path takes care of practical matters and offers an axis for planning plantings on either side. In this case, the tree and containers balance but don't mirror a flower bed that offers color and interest.

This one-story bungalow was surrounded by towering trees in its established neighborhood, but it needed some low-lying color to frame the house and keep the focus on it. Colorful ground covers and a puzzle of a path do just that.

Balance practical needs with aesthetic ones before you finalize a landscape plan. Ample lawn and an easily accessible porch meet this family's needs; a series of mounding plants define and separate the activity areas.

evaluating your needs

● ● ● A SEAMLESS AESTHETIC IS IMPORTANT, BUT there are other practical matters to consider. For instance, how much time are you willing to spend on maintenance? What's the right balance for your family between front-yard privacy and being neighborly? What existing trees and hardscape features (such as driveways, paths, fences) do you need to factor in? How large is your lot and what special issues do you need to work around? Before you make a single purchase, make a list of problems that could be solved or improvements that could be made that would make your environment a better fit for your family. Call a family meeting and get everyone's input (and buy-in) in a brainstorming session.

QUESTIONS TO CONSIDER

here is a list of common questions professional landscapers ask before they embark on a plan of action.

1. **Look out your windows and doors to the front yard.** Are there views you'd like to screen…or frame? Would you like to perk up your view from the living room with a colorful front garden? Would you like more privacy screening for a front bedroom?

2. **Check out your house from the street.** What's your general impression about the style and color? Does it appear too stark? Could it use some color? Are overgrown plants blocking paths or architectural elements? Are there features you'd like to accent better?

3. **Walk around your front yard.** How is the space shaped? Are all the edges of your property straight lines and corners? Is there an easy route from the drive to the door and from the street to the door? Are there any areas that need work, such as crumbling steps or overgrown shrubs?

4. **Take note of how you feel in your yard.** Is it too exposed or do you feel too closed off from the neighbors? Is it a pleasant atmosphere, with fragrance and natural buffers against sound? Are there interesting places for your eyes to rest?

5. **Look at the land.** Is it flat, sloped, or rolling? Could a retaining wall give you more usable lawn? Is drainage a problem that could be corrected by redoing the landscape? Is the soil well nourished?

6. **Inspect existing plantings.** Are they healthy and attractive or do certain plants need to be pruned, moved, or removed? Do the plants offer all-season interest? Do you have too much—or too little—variety?

7. **Look at how the light falls on your property.** Do you get full sun, complete shade, or a mix of the two? Are there heavily shaded areas where nothing seems to grow? Does your house get too much sunlight or too little? Which direction does your house face?

8. **Think about how weather affects your house.** Does your house need to be screened from strong winter winds? Could your paths be easier to shovel in snow? Do the entryways to your home need more protection?

9. **Drive around your neighborhood, community, and even the surrounding countryside.** What plants, construction materials, and landscaping styles distinguish your region from other parts of the country? What ideas do you like that would be right for your site and neighborhood?

10. **Evaluate your property at night.** Do paths and steps need to be better illuminated for safety? Can you see to back your car down the driveway and into the street?

creating your plan

● ● ● GRAB SOME GRAPH PAPER AND A PENCIL to try your hand at planning on paper. You don't have to be Picasso to make a simple scale drawing of your house and property, you just need to be handy with a ruler. By doing this you'll get a clearer sense of the proportion of front yard to house to consider and how many different elements you have to work around.

A landscape plan allows you to play with ideas and change your mind before you grab the garden tools. A plan is also a great communication tool when more than one person is invested in the outcome. Finally, a plan lets you place elements thoughtfully. This is especially important for picking plant materials, as you'll be able to factor in their size at full growth.

By drawing a rough site plan, you can determine what space you have available to balance soft elements, such as shrubs and flowering plants, with hardscape features, such as steps, a driveway, and even a flagpole.

Even the smallest of lots can include multiple layers of interest. This tiny cottage has a welcoming front yard that bursts with hydrangea and soft greenery.

more about...
DRAWING A SIMPLE LANDSCAPE PLAN

simple bubble diagram can help you visualize what a final plan will look like. Draw existing elements to scale on graph paper, including your house, driveway, and any other hardscape features. Draw in any new features you are considering, being careful to illustrate trees or shrubs at full height. Draw up several different approaches and get some feedback from other family members. This is also a handy communication tool to take to a landscape expert. The point is to think through the changes on paper before you pick up a shovel.

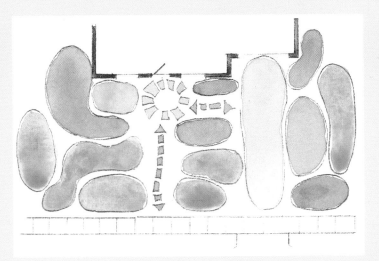

consider the neighborhood

● ● ● AS YOU ARE THINKING ABOUT WHAT KIND of plantings and features will perk up your front yard, you have at least two important factors to consider as well… your neighbors. Fences and fast-growing hedges do make good neighbors, but only as long as the fence blends visually with the architecture and the hedge is trimmed neatly.

Creating a more diversified front landscape can be an inspiration to the neighborhood with its thoughtful and appropriate design. It's also a commitment to maintenance. So before you plant a front perennial bed or create a courtyard water fountain, think about how much time you realistically have to devote to its upkeep.

In neighborhoods marked by traditional architecture, a formal, green-only garden blends beautifully with the environment and is the easiest to keep in line with regular pruning.

RIGHT Border plantings and low stone walls not only define property lines, but they also enhance the whole neighborhood with color and dimension.

FACING PAGE Front gardens are a beautiful thing, as long as they're properly maintained. Brick pathways act like garden edging to keep this perennial garden within its boundaries.

heck your municipality's rules on planting within the parking strip (that sliver of land between the road and the sidewalk). Some communities have restrictions about how tall plants can be for instance, or how far away you should plant from a fire hydrant.

Every state has some version of the "one call" law, requiring homeowners and professional contractors to have utility lines marked before any digging takes place. This rule usually leaves out digging with hand tools. But if you are planting large trees, sinking posts for a porch, or doing any landscaping that requires mechanical equipment, don't forget to call before you dig.

let color lead the way

COORDINATING A COLOR PALETTE BETWEEN your home and yard creates a more cohesive design and artful appearance. The house colors that are easiest to integrate are the greens, browns, and beiges of nature. When a house already blends with the surrounding landscape, flowers or stonework are needed only for a hint of contrast. In this case, most colors will work. But to keep the look seamless, choose no more than three accent colors for contrast.

Bright house colors are dramatic and should be paired with equally bold colors in a front garden. Muted house colors—those with a lot of gray in them—are enhanced by hues that have similarly dusky colors.

A pastel-painted house is a natural backdrop for the soft shades and sparkling greens of flowering plants, shrubs, and trees. Cool colors, such as blue, green or gray, get a visual lift from foliage and flowers in similar colors, just as apricot, red, or yellow houses spark to warm shades of plant life. If you prefer the punch of contrasting colors, mix cool colors (blues and greens) with warm ones (reds and yellows) to liven things up.

ABOVE Mixed greens, including silvery lamb's ear and wispy prairie grass, cue from the mossy green of the home. Burgundy trim inspired flowering plants in deep purple and reddish pinks.

RIGHT The soft yellow of evening primrose softens this white cottage, while the white snow daisies link the house to its rural landscape.

FACING PAGE Use consistent color to tie together your landscape and link it to your house. Flowering purple plants, such as salvia and catmint, make these beds feel connected and draw the eye to the focal point element—the house.

21

Houses clad in beiges or browns are the easiest to color coordinate. Here, drifts of variegated grasses, lavender plants, and burgundy bushes add rich color without overwhelming the neutral house.

A white-on-white scheme can be fresh and pretty. For visual success, break up the white with plenty of green elements, such as this boxwood hedge.

Rich green foliage adds color and contrast to any white or pale home. A mix of free-flowing and trimmed greenery softens the edges of this squared-off house.

BELOW A row of Calla lilies echoes the crisp white trim of this bungalow. Then, a mix of fresh greens in chartreuse, burgundy, and evergreen links to (and perks up) the home's sage-color clapboard.

MORE COLORFUL SCHEMES

nspiration is all around you. By flipping through this book and other landscape and garden publications you'll get a sense of the endless color combinations that exist between façades and front beds. If you aren't ready for a color change on your house, enhance the existing color with harmonious, eye-pleasing landscape materials. Take your cues from the trim paint or even the roof color, as well as from the house's primary color, and weave these into your front-yard plan to tie the two together. Let these common house colors and potential planting schemes spur your own ideas.

NEUTRAL TERRITORY

Neutrals, such as beige, green, and gray, are the easiest colors to plant against because they blend with so many colors. Just think of how versatile your khaki pants are! Draw from your home's trim or roof color when you want to add the pop of contrast. A classic color scheme would include violet blue, soft rosy red, lavender, and yellow plantings. Avoid too many bold, jarring colors.

CLASSIC WHITES

White houses can appear cold and bland without a layering of texture and color. Use an abundance of white in your scheme to link the house more fully with its landscape. Pastel yellows, pinks, and purples will soften the setting, where deep jewel tones might pop off a white backdrop too harshly. Foliage that is blue, silver, or variegated also complements white.

MELLOW YELLOWS

Almost any color pairs well with a sunny yellow. Purple and lavender are contrasting colors, so use them to add drama and energy. Or play with a palette of oranges and yellow-greens for more harmony and calm. Use foliage variegated with creams and golds to weave more yellow into the landscape.

BRICK REDS

Red- or brown-tinged brick brightens with hot oranges, yellows, and scarlet, or even the more mellow peach-pinks and soft yellows. Avoid cool lavenders or pinks because they will clash with the brick. Switch instead to violet-blue flowers or burgundy foliage.

BROWNS

Many colors work well with easygoing, neutral brown. Using a mix of pale and deep pinks and yellow, along with burgundy foliage, will conjure a rich but mellow feeling. Purples or reds don't pop off deep brown as readily but will be fine as accents.

BLUES

When planting against a blue house, don't be afraid to go for some contrast. Choose soft oranges, coppery shades, or golden yellows to bring energy to your front yard. Or opt for complementary shades of lavender, blue, and purple for a calming scheme. Silver or blue-green foliage makes subtle accents, while burgundy isn't as easy to integrate.

when to hire a professional

● ● ● THE FRONT YARD OFFERS MANY WAYS FOR a do-it-yourselfer to build a little sweat equity in a property. On the other hand, since landscape design is an art and a science that involves design, horticulture, and construction, it often makes sense to call in a professional for major makeovers. Get a professional involved for help with the overall concept, for planting plans, at the construction phase, or for all stages of your project. Whether you hire a landscape designer, landscape architect, or garden designer depends on the scope of your project and your own skill level.

Many companies that sell landscape materials also offer design services. This is a good way to find a designer to help you with a plan, leaving you with the option of doing the installation yourself to save money. Or ask for referrals from neighbors whose landscape catches your eye. Local nurseries are another good source to find garden designers and other professionals. Ask to see samples of their work and references you can follow up on. Find out whether their specialty is space planning, hardscaping, or working with plants. Ask about the scope of services they provide and how they bill for them. For more extensive projects you should see a concept or site plan.

If your landscape plan includes constructing retaining walls and filling in a large lot, consider tapping into the talents of a landscape professional. Here, a series of well-placed planting beds and a cobblestone retaining wall finish off this new, but traditionally styled, home.

This cobblestone cottage was special enough in and of itself. But a new portico and lush foundation plantings gave more strength to the surroundings for a nestled-in look.

more about...
WHICH EXPERT TO CALL

LANDSCAPE ARCHITECT

If you are installing a driveway, rebuilding your front porch, or situating a new home on a lot, a landscape architect is the one to call. Most states license landscape architects, who generally have advanced degrees in their field. Many are members of the American Society of Landscape Architects (ASLA). Contact this organization for referrals in your area.

LANDSCAPE DESIGNER

Most landscape designers are not licensed but have studied design and horticulture and are certified by

the Association of Professional Landscape Designers (APLD). This type of professional most often specializes in residential design and can help you create a master plan, help you address trouble spots in your landscape, and install plantings and beds.

GARDEN DESIGNER

This design professional focuses on creating gardens and working with plants rather than on an overall landscape plan. Though they don't have a governing body, a garden designer many be just what you need for small-scale projects that don't involve a lot of hardscaping.

making an entrance

● ○ ○

WHAT'S THE CLOSEST WAY TO GET FROM YOUR FRONT SEAT TO YOUR front door? Chart it out and you've got the perfect passageway to create a nice, easy transition from the outside world to your inner sanctum. If you're looking for a front-yard change that is big on impact and small on hassle, the entry is the place to start. Perhaps you have the path and the porch, but you just need some softening and style to make it more welcoming and memorable. Maybe you need to turn a naturally worn footpath into something more permanent or to convert a small stoop into a more pleasant landing pad for guests waiting to enter or pausing to say goodbye.

Take a good hard look at your entry. Think about both practical and aesthetic aspects of this bridge to your home. Does it extend a gracious welcome? Or is it cold and stark, lacking in color, texture, or dimension that pleases the eye and softens the sharp angles of your house? On the practical side, is there a covered place for guests to stand? Are your house numbers visible from the street, and can visitors find the way easily and safely to your door once darkness falls?

Details count here. Paint your door a fresh color to create a focal point to guide your guests. Arrange a few colorful plant containers on a small stoop and see what a little touch of nature does as a softening agent. For more ambitious change, consider adding a columned portico or extending a stoop into a full-fledged porch. These changes will not only improve your home's appearance, but also will pump up your home's enjoyment factor as well.

A subtly arching barrel vault and simple columns create a portico that gives this traditional two story a more dimensional look while offering visitors a protected place to stand. A center path flanked by long-blooming coneflowers and easy-to-grow grasses underscores the thoughtful welcome.

porches and porticos

● ● ● ALMOST ALL HOUSES COME COMPLETE with a covered entry, whether it's a porch that spans the front of the structure or a small stoop topped with a portico or awning. Depending on the climate, these features perform practical roles, offering temporary shelter against the elements and, in the case of the porch, an extension of living space into the outdoors. And they perform a design function as well, framing the entry and lending architectural interest.

If your house seems a little too boxy or has a flat, featureless façade, consider how you might build its character by layering on a porch or portico. For instance, you can add to what you have, extending a front stoop into a more accommodating terrace. If you plan on building a structure into your front-yard landscaping, be sure to check your local building codes before you put your plan in motion. There are codes that dictate setbacks, the distance from the road to the structure, as well as those that deal with the ratio between the size of the lot and structure on it.

Perennials of different heights and climbing vines frame this bungalow in a charming way and add privacy to the porch. A flagstone courtyard provides a spot to enjoy the garden from both sides.

ABOVE Plantings support the symmetry of this traditional stone house, cutting a beautiful walkway that leads from path to porch to portico.

A porch doesn't have to wrap around or even extend the length of the house to provide architectural charm or a place to rock. When set along the edge of the porch instead of below a window, a window box adds privacy and a sense of enclosure.

ESSENTIAL ELEMENTS OF AN INVITING ENTRY

A CLEAR PATH

Save the meandering paths for the backyard, where you want to linger and explore. A path to your front door should be obvious, even if it turns here and there. Paths should be wide enough for two people to walk together. This also leaves room for plants to spill over the edges without getting your ankles wet with morning dew.

COLOR

Rather than having just a swath of green foundation plantings, inject a little color in the form of vibrant flowers or a brightly painted object, such as a bench. Paint the bench the same color as the front door to tie the bench visually to the house.

CONTAINERS AND ORNAMENTS

Give your guests a preview of your personality, and give yourself some familiar objects to welcome you home. Start with a beautiful container, birdbath, or fountain. These objects bridge the gap between the house and the garden.

SUFFICIENT LIGHTING

While you could find your door in the darkness without too much trouble, it's nearly impossible for your guests. Pathway lighting and an attractive front light near the door make nighttime visitors feel warmly welcomed. Blazing safety lights, however, are off-putting.

•the front porch

The front porch has a history that reaches back to the early days of this country. Before the advent of air-conditioning, the porch was the all-in-one, open-air living area where dining, relaxing, and entertaining took place during sweltering summers. Porches brought neighbors together and helped us relax—both ourselves and our decorating. Next to Grandma's attic, the front porch may be the most romantic space in the home, given its prominent role in American culture, literature, and history.

Somewhere during the postwar building boom of the 1950s and 1960s, the porch was written off the floor plan. Both houses and landscapes were simplified to keep up with demand for new housing, and we retreated to private back patios (usually a large, square slab of cement) when we needed a fresh-air fix. Now porches, like front-yard landscaping, are making a comeback. Culturally, we are longing for more connections to nature, to our neighborhoods, and to our own past. But on a more personal level, there is nothing quite like a breezy front porch to help us slow down and experience simple pleasure, just as there is nothing quite like the front porch as a charming transition from world to home.

A front porch without railings or roof? Sure, especially when a covered porch would overwhelm a small home. This simple wood decking gives owners a place to enjoy their front garden without blocking light in to the front windows.

ABOVE Terraces are porches that have a paved or tiled floor. Combine this type of flooring with intricate wrought-iron railings and detailing to conjure sunny, Mediterranean style.

TOP RIGHT In keeping with the modern style of this custom-built home, the front porch is made with unconventional materials, including the cable railings and exposed brackets. Ordinary slats mask the area between the porch deck and the yard in a creative way.

BOTTOM RIGHT Traditional front porches typically are built above ground level, accessible by steps. Plant greenery that will grow at least to the height of the porch floor to soften and underscore this architectural asset.

33

porticos in practice

In simple terms, a portico is a covering for a porch or walkway that is supported by columns. Porticos give a finished look to a home's entry while putting a little roof over the heads of people trying to get in the front door. Porticos also add a note of classical style to a residence, giving it a sense of grandeur.

Adding a portico might be as easy as covering an existing stoop or landing with an awning or structure that is in keeping with your home's architecture. For a seamless addition, use the same materials on the portico that are on the roof and select a column style that matches the mood of your house.

ABOVE A portico can make a dramatic style statement. This post-and-beam entry—constructed of wood and stone in their natural state—introduces this house's Arts-and-Crafts design.

Supported by simple and elegant Tuscan-style columns, this square portico adds the right amount of grandeur to this traditional home. Symmetrical foundation plantings frame the entrance without marring its clean, formal look.

Covered walkways supported by columns are technically porticos, too. This one links up garage and house with architectural flair, while offering protection and a clear path to the front door.

more about ...
COLUMN MATERIALS

Wood It can be fluted, carved, turned, and tapered into classic columns of all types. But wood is also susceptible to weather and insect damage, so it demands the most upkeep of all the column materials.

Stone Nothing beats the strength and permanence of stone, but this material is the most costly of all the column options.

Composite Stone Made from superdurable polyester resins, composite stone columns have the look and feel of real stone but at a fraction of the cost—and weight—of cast stone because they can be made hollow.

PVC and Fiberglass New construction materials are low- to no-maintenance at less cost than most wood columns. They're easier to install, which cuts construction costs.

Column Wraps Designed to install around an existing support, column wraps are a good option for masking damaged or unattractive columns in an affordable way. Made of PVC or fiberglass, the wraps are maintenance free and easy for a homeowner with average do-it-yourself skills to install.

entry doors

The right entry door puts a punctuation mark on a home's style statement. Design an entry that is in keeping with the style and the size of your home to avoid a discordant feeling that will fight the warm welcome you're trying to achieve. Make this architectural feature a focal point by painting it a contrasting color. Flank it with glistening sidelights or top it with a frieze to call attention to the entry door and give your house more architectural dimension and a finished look.

Colonial-style doors feature pilasters (flat side columns) topped by a pediment for a clean and classical look.

ABOVE **Match the charming simplicity of a bungalow with a straightforward, raised-panel door. The clean style of the sidelights complements the four-pane windows.**

Modern houses have a "less is more" aesthetic. This custom entry door, in chic black, has undecorated frosted glass panels and stripped-down hardware.

Warm wood doors are a natural complement to brick and stone houses. A single sidelight is less formal than a double treatment and is in keeping with the cottage feeling.

BELOW The honey tones and natural graining of this solid-wood door complement the home's stucco exterior. Its simple design would work with many traditional home styles.

the courtyard approach

● ● ● THE COMFORT A COURTYARD OFFERS makes it a compelling option for homes today: privacy, tranquility, and a buffered zone in which to enjoy light, air, and the beauty of your natural surroundings.

A courtyard can be as simple or complex as you want to make it. Small trees, shrubs, and walls offer relief from the sun, wind, and noise. You don't need a wraparound building to carve out a courtyard; even low walls or hedges offer a sense of enclosure and a cozy atmosphere. When designing a courtyard, think about how your family will use the space. Should it be big enough for al fresco dining? Or are you looking only for enough space to enjoy the morning paper?

There are an endless number of ways to define a courtyard. Narrow down the options by factoring in your house style, your budget, and your time frame. The least expensive way to enclose an area is with a hedge, a border of grasses, or other favorite plantings. You can also consider trellises, fences, stone walls...or a mix of all of the above. When it comes to flooring, look for materials that complement the architectural style of your home. Remember that if calm is what you're after, keep contrast and clutter to a minimum.

U-shape houses offer a ready niche to create a simple courtyard entry. The wings of this house flank a poured-cement landing that—with the addition of a couple of comfortable chairs and some grasses for screening—offer an open-air hideaway.

Chart a pleasant journey to your front door with a courtyard entry garden. This courtyard
uses a mix of flooring materials to define activity areas and add to the sense of discovery.

Don't let a small area stop you from adding courtyard romance to your front yard. Lush plantings wrap around a small brick patio on this tiny city lot.

ABOVE Create a courtyard in a weekend by piecing together irregular chunks of slate or flagstone. Build from an existing walkway or stoop to connect the courtyard to its surroundings.

LEFT Courtyards give a front exterior an appealing layered look. This townhouse would look bare without the clever use of picket fencing and a raised-brick courtyard.

entry gardens

●●● A HOUSE IS MADE OF LINES, ANGLES, AND flat surfaces that can come off as cold and stark, so throw your home's façade a few soft curves with flower beds, climbing greenery, and garden color. Gardens are no longer banished to the backyard because of their ability to link a home to its natural setting and give it a settled-in, finished look. The best part? Even homeowners with little do-it-yourself skill or inclination can sink plant life into the ground and enjoy the dramatic improvement that results.

From simple pathways bordered with blooms to flowering courtyards, how extensive your entry garden becomes is up to you. Before you plant, think about how much time you have to devote to maintenance. Choose plants based on how well they will thrive in their setting. Consider light levels, soil composition, and climate. The goal is to plant a lush garden that frames your entry with color and texture. Straggly, struggling plants just won't have the same effect.

Flowers planted around a front entry skirt a house with color and texture. The soft purples and pinks of this perennial garden enliven the gray exterior.

Use long-blooming,
carefree roses for
height and mass plus
a season's worth
of color. Once big
plants are in place,
fill in around them
with low-growing
euphorbia and
fragrant herbs.

Underscore the charm of a cottage exterior with a loose and colorful flower
garden. Oversize stepping stones and curved, white fencing echo the home's
architecture for a finished look.

•flowering front entries

Engage all the senses and create a welcoming border between your lawn and your doorstep by softening a path with plant life. The strip between front path and foundation makes a natural flower bed, creating an opportunity for you to turn an ordinary walkway into a more interesting and colorful journey. Flank a center path with flowers and lighting, and you've also outlined a clear and colorful map to your front door—a path that, at its best, underscores your home's style and your family's personality.

As you plan your plantings, think about how your entry will look through the seasons. Include perennials that bloom in succession throughout the growing season. Add fall and winter interest with berried shrubs and evergreens. If you need a buffer for privacy and protection from the elements, consider planting tall grasses and small trees on both sides of the walkway. If you plan for function and a visual connection to your architecture, you're on your way to creating a grand entrance, no matter how small it is in stature.

Ornamental evergreens and space-filling sedums make an artful and unique addition to a modern ranch house. The plantings are low maintenance and high texture...a good mix.

Lush with annuals, perennials, and evergreens planted within the space from sidewalk to front porch, this entryway signals an exuberant welcome.

t o discourage weeds and encourage a more natural-looking walkway, look into hardy perennials that creep into the voids between stepping-stone or brick paths. Above the ground, the plants will soften the look and feel of the path, while below ground level, their roots will prevent erosion.

Here are three plants to try that will hold up under heavy foot traffic:

Woolly Thyme grows in low and flat branches, perfect for extending its reach over solid pathways or stones. In midsummer, this decorative thyme pops with mauve flowers.

Blue Star Creeper appears delicate with tiny blue blossoms that open up in midsummer, but it can handle being walked on. Be sure to put boundaries around this robust creeper.

Brass Buttons has foliage that looks like miniature fern fronds. It grows in a solid mat that prevents weed growth. You'll need to sink a hard edging at least 2 inches thick to keep it in its place.

A curved path from the driveway to the front door of this new suburban home is softened up with a mix of waving grasses, long-blooming roses, and other natural elements that graciously mark the way and add layering to the house.

Entry gardens are a pretty option for places that are tough to mow. On this postage-stamp lot, a delicate spring garden extends a gracious welcome. The same flowers are planted both inside and outside the fence so the small lot doesn't look chopped up.

The geometric design of this entry path leaves cutouts for tidy garden beds that suit the home's formal demeanor. A container and bench mark the transitions in the path.

ABOVE Border a walkway with mixed annuals for a mosaic of color that lasts all season. This tumble of blooms makes a cheerful, exuberant expression that hints at the personality of the homeowners.

Play with line and form to create an artful front yard. It's clear that creative spirits live in this house. Plant an entry garden in sections with a lot of repetition for eye-pleasing design rhythm and a cleaner, more contemporary look.

A WELCOMING GARDEN

garden designer Gordon Haywood thought a lot about the role of entry gardens in his book *The Welcoming Garden: Designing Your Own Front Garden*. Here he shares his insights.

Q : What is a "welcoming garden"?

A : The term defines the entrance garden in front of the house, the ground where we say, "Welcome to my home." I'm trying to imply the notion of engaging people with fragrances to smell, textures to experience, and interesting plants and sculpture to look at as they move to the house's front door. Whenever I design a garden, I start at the front of the house. That's where you define the style of the garden in light of the house. If you see the entrance garden as an extension of the home rather than as a means to pretty up the place, you're on your way to creating a welcoming entryway.

Q : What's the first step in creating an entry garden?

A : Start with an assessment of your views. Stand at the front door and then at the inside windows that look out on to the front. Do you see a lot of driveway? Do you see a lot of the street? Do you see cars going by? Where do people park their cars, and what route takes them to the front door? Then walk out to the street or driveway and assess the view of your entryway from there. Ask yourself, "Does the house feel warm and welcoming?"

Q : What elements create a welcoming garden?

A : If you plant both sides of the path that leads to your front door—and nothing else—you've made a good

start creating a welcoming garden. Take colors you've used inside and bring them outside—in annuals, perennials, foliage, and objects like outdoor sculptures and pots, which can hint at the life lived indoors. A gardener who collects modern art might place a sleek granite sculpture out front. Outdoor furniture might also echo the interior style. The relationship between inside and outside goes right to the heart of "welcome."

Q : What roles do containers play?

A : A good entrance garden should provide a number of engaging, calming experiences as you walk from the driveway to the front door; containers can help by marking the transitional points. Each experience you have along the path to the front door helps you leave behind the tense world of driving, traffic, stoplights, etc., so that you arrive at the front door calm.

Q : It sounds as if moving through the entrance garden becomes an experience, a journey where you don't mind pausing.

A : Right. An entrance garden is what you are offering your guests as they leave the world of traffic, angry drivers on cell phones, and navigating right or left. Your garden is the calming influence; it's the exhaling.

LEFT To design a garden that is more earthy than exuberant, select plant life that gets its beauty from foliage rather than flowers. Leaves of different colors, types, and textures add subtle interest without overwhelming the home's natural shake and soft green exterior.

BELOW Pull plantings away from the foundation to give your entry dimension and a sense of journey. Here, freeform roses counter the straight lines of a boxwood hedge to create more interest and to define the entry path.

LEFT Low-growing ferns and dwarf grasses naturalize. To discourage weeds and encourage a more natural looking walkway, look into hardy perennials that creep into the voids between stepping-stone or brick paths. Go beyond the standard ground covers to those that can tolerate foot traffic and keep growing strong. Above the ground, the plants will soften the look and feel of the path, while below ground level, their roots will prevent erosion.

arbor ideas

● ● ● ANOTHER WAY TO ADD SHELTER AND dimension to your front entry is with a well-placed arbor. Unlike porticos or porches, these freestanding elements are easy to add and affordable. Though an arbor, granted, won't keep your guests dry in a rainstorm, it does offer shade, architectural interest, and a sense of privacy. Place an arbor over a path as a guidepost for your guests or to highlight an entry. Add color by hanging containers from an arbor, or plant climbing vines to tether an arbor more fully to its surroundings. Plant several different vines with varying bloom times so you—and your visitors—can enjoy color and fragrance throughout the season.

Placed midway along a front walk, an arbor adds a sense of fun and romance to the journey. Frothy with white rose blooms, this arbor enhances the home's cottage feel.

Frame a plain front door with an arbor, and you've got an instant portico. This arbor is affixed to a wooden stoop to boost it to above-door height.

Arbors make a dramatic entrance and frame a front-yard view. This arbor is placed at the point where the driveway meets the front path to mark the transition.

Though most arbors are arched, there are arbors of all styles and shapes. Echoing the home's rafters, this substantial gabled arbor pairs well with the Arts-and-Crafts style of the home.

paths and driveways

● ● ●

PATHS AND DRIVEWAYS ARE HARDWORKING ELEMENTS IN A FRONT landscape. When well designed and constructed, they guide you to where you need to be and get you there safely. But given the sheer amount of visual space these supporting players take up in a front-yard scheme, it's smart to factor in how path and drive materials look as well as how they perform.

The materials you choose for paths and driveways—known in the business as the "hardscape" elements in your front yard—can set the mood you want for your home. A meandering brick path that's edged with flowers offers a warm greeting that seems to say: "Relax, slow down, and enjoy the journey." Straight-edge surfaces that present a more direct route have a more formal feeling.

Driveway materials can be chosen to complement the style and color of your exterior. At the very least, think about materials that won't detract from the overall design of your front yard. With new manufactured materials hitting the market, there are more options than you might think. Considering the amount of space—and budget—the driveway gobbles up, it pays to research all of your options before the bulldozer arrives.

Match the color and mood of your paths and drives to your house to underscore your home's style. When this couple added on to their 1920s-era home, they added a classic brick drive and pathway to blend the existing structure with the addition.

planning for pathways

● ● ● EVEN BEFORE YOU CONSIDER HOW FRONT pathways look, think about how you live. If this path is the primary route to your home, one you'll travel laden with groceries, small children, or homework from the office, a smooth and straight pathway is your best course. If this is your "forever home," or you need to consider visitors with special needs, there are pathway materials and designs that will ease the transition but still look lovely. Not one for yard work? Consider how easy the path is to mow around in the summer and shovel in the winter.

A straight path that finds the shortest route between drive and door is the easiest and least expensive route to take. But this straightforward approach can also make visitors feel rushed... especially if it lacks visual interest along the way. A curved path leaves time for experiencing the highlights of your front landscape, and it has more inherent charm. Zigzagging paths represent a good compromise between the two, adding design interest and a greater sense of adventure along the way.

Once your lifestyle and safety issues are factored in, think about how the path will look in the context of your house and yard. If possible, match the colors and materials to your architecture. A brick path or a concrete path edged in brick is an obvious choice for a brick house. A flagstone path easily complements a home with a stone foundation. If the choice isn't as obvious, think about matching your hardscape with roofing or trim colors. A natural slate path makes a good companion to a home with dark gray shingles, for instance, because of how the color will link the two elements into a cohesive whole.

Stretching directly from sidewalk to front door, the straight center path approach is the most formal front walkway. In a classic herringbone pattern, this gated brick pathway suits this traditional center-hall, two-story home.

Take cues from your home's architectural style and materials to pick pathway materials. With enchanting charm, this irregular flagstone path guides visitors in from the street.

By using the same shade of stone, but varying the type, shape, or texture, you'll add interest without busyness. Cut into uniform rectangles, this jagged bluestone path neatly links to the cobblestone foundation—but with a fun "edge."

m o r e   a b o u t ...
GRAVEL PATHS

gravel is the easiest and least expensive surface option for pathways, making it a do-it-yourselfer's dream. Here's how to get one done:

1. Determine your path's design and width by using two garden hoses to mark potential routes. Consider drainage as you plan. Remember a main path to your home should be at least 4 feet wide.

2. Finalize the design and use an edger or spade to mark the walkway. Remove the hoses.

3. Dig out 4 to 6 inches of topsoil from the path; clear any roots.

4. Place plastic or steel edging along the outer edges of the path, securing it with pins or spikes.

5. Cover the pathway with landscape fabric.

6. Cover with 2 to 3 inches of sand and pack down firmly with shovel or drum roller.

7. Top off with a 2- to 3-inch layer of pea gravel, wood chips, mulch, river pebbles, or standard gravel.

8. Rake smooth.

•one path or two?

A front walkway that stretches from the driveway to the front entry isn't the only path to take. The guiding question is: Where do your visitors most often park? If there is ample room to park in the driveway, a single path might do. If driveway parking is limited, a center path from the street to the house might be more useful. Often, two paths make the most sense—one that originates at the driveway and a second that starts at the sidewalk. Another option for narrow driveways is to add a path alongside the drive that can be used when cars fill the main surface.

Think of your walkway as the red carpet you roll out for your family and friends. Consider the type of welcome you want to create as well as the ease and experience of the journey for all. It's possible to underestimate the importance of a pathway, until you stop to consider how often it's used and who will be using it.

ABOVE Brick pathways knit brick houses tightly to their setting, visually expanding the size of the house. This pathway and courtyard make a wide and welcoming entrance to the cozy, brick Tudor house.

RIGHT Spare modern homes could be cobbled up with busy stonework. These owners cleverly echoed the slats of their home's façade by building a boardwalk from the street and the driveway.

CLASSIC BRICKWORK PATTERNS

the following are some of the most common brick patterns. Stick with one pattern for a formal look, or mix it up for a casual feel or to highlight changes in function. For instance, switch patterns when a path shifts into a patio or courtyard.

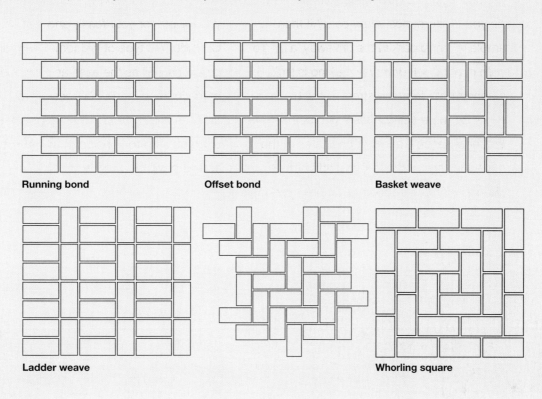

Running bond

Offset bond

Basket weave

Ladder weave

Whorling square

Adding multiple paths is one good way of cutting down on yard work. In this classic New England shingle house, a wide path made with pavers links up with auxiliary paths with similar, but smaller, pavers to provide easy access to the house.

materials for walkways

●●● THANKS TO ADVANCES IN MANUFACTURED stone and composite materials, there are more surface choices than ever before. Pavers made of concrete are stronger than poured concrete and can be made to look like brick or stone. Stone is just as versatile and varied, and it can be cut to fit the angles and curves of a pathway. Even ordinary concrete is being tinted, stamped, and studded, allowing homeowners to add decorative flair to this otherwise nondescript material.

Secure footing should be the main goal of a walkway. Consider your climate and these two practical matters before you make your material choice: how slippery the material gets when wet and how hot it gets when the sun is shining. Polished or honed stone can be tricky to navigate when it's wet. Alternately, natural stone and concrete absorb the heat from the sun, making exposed paths too hot for comfort if you like to go barefoot or if children use it for a play area.

more about...
SELECTING A PATHWAY MATERIAL

brick is very durable and can range in color from deep red to sandy yellow. The glazing process determines whether brick is rough and matte or slightly glossy in finish. Bricks also vary in thickness. The most common bricks for paths or patios are twice as thick as those intended for facing a wall or fireplace. You can also shop for recycled brick, which breaks up the uniformity in favor of added character.

Stone is another durable option. This natural, of-the-earth material helps a landscape appear more established. One of the best—and most common—stones for walkways is flagstone. This stone is irregularly shaped but evenly layered, so it can be split into slabs. Bluestone, slate, and sandstone are all types of flagstone. Many of these stones are sold as cut pavers, which come as square or rectangular pieces of even thickness that can be laid more easily. Flagstones, like brick, can be either dry-laid or mortared.

Concrete pavers are less expensive than stone and brick, but they can mimic those natural materials. Made from poured concrete and available mixed with a variety of other aggregates, they can be cast into interesting shapes or cut and laid into a variety of patterns. Concrete pavers can also be tinted into a candy-store assortment of colors. Concrete pavers do not require mortar and are three times stronger than poured concrete. Best of all, they shift without cracking as soil conditions change, making them ideal for cold-weather climates.

Poured concrete is smooth and subtle...unless you don't want it to be! It can be pigmented, stained, textured, scored, or combined with aggregate (composed of rock fragments) for more design flair. Because this poured material has more design flexibility, it can be used in combination with stone, bricks, or pavers for unique effects.

pathways

Inset poured concrete into a brick
framework for a unique combination
that also saves cost.

Sandstone's creamy shades and
soft graining blends with many
different exteriors.

continued on page 60

pathways (continued)

ABOVE LEFT Recycled materials, such as these railroad ties, make clever pathways, especially when mixed with other options.

ABOVE RIGHT Poured and cast pavers look like brick and stone but are easier to work with and more durable than the real thing.

These square concrete pavers are textured to blend more readily into their gravel bed.

Tinted concrete makes an artful frame for a mortared path of flagstones made from bluestone.

Sink natural stone to ground level to achieve a naturalized feeling, like the woodlands effect of this well-placed bluestone.

steps and slopes

● ● ● UNLESS YOUR PROPERTY IS FLAT, YOU'LL have to decide whether steps or a sloped path offers the safest route to your entry. If you have a 6 percent or less grade change (measured as a 3-inch change over a 4-foot length of ground), then you're better off with a gently sloping pathway. Sloping walkways are easier to negotiate and install.

If your grade change is steeper than 6 percent, you'll need to plan for steps. An even sharper grade change requires steps and retaining walls that need to be designed carefully. For this job, think about calling in a landscape professional, who will likely recommend avoiding long runs of steps without a landing, if the grade is not too steep to provide for it. A landing serves two purposes: it offers both a resting stop for users and a stabilizer for the steps.

If you're designing your own steps, safety is key. The goal is to create a rise-to-run ratio that most people will be able to take with a natural stride. Good combinations include a 5½-inch rise with a 15-inch tread, a 6½-inch rise with a 14-inch tread, and a 4½-inch rise with a 17-inch tread. For safety reasons, keep this ratio consistent throughout the length of the path and be sure to add proper lighting. If you have three or more steps, you'll also have to factor in a handrail.

For houses on lots with little or no grade, a gently sloping path might work. This mortared flagstone path leads right to the home's threshold for a safe and accessible approach.

For houses perched higher than the street, steps are a necessity. Use the same or similar material as the foundation to create steps that blend into the architecture.

Steps designed with low risers and deep treads will be easier for most people to navigate. Though steep enough to require a retaining wall, these gradually rising steps operate more like a sloping path.

Rectangular pavers make naturalized stair risers. These pavers were carefully sited to keep them level in this home's secondary pathway.

• materials for steps

Poured concrete, flagstone, and brick are all good choices for steps. Aggregate can be added to concrete to improve its surface friction. A slightly textured flagstone (limestone or sandstone, for instance) will be a better choice than a solid-surface stone (such as slate). In a rustic setting, recycled railroad ties can be used, but they require more maintenance to keep the fill behind them level and the risers even.

For a long run of steps where landings are involved, consider changing the materials to call attention to the transitions. For instance, add a row of brick to concrete steps, or for all-brick steps, change the pattern or direction of the brick to signal a change. Lining the steps with boulders or fieldstones is another good way to highlight a shift from steps to flat landing.

Poured concrete pavers and steps are the least expensive materials for crafting steps and pathways. Here, in its most unadorned form, the humble material makes a modern statement.

Earthy but classic brick makes an easy transition from pathway to stairway. A partial brick wall marks the shift from path to stair landing and screens the stairway to prevent it from becoming too strong an element.

Extend a standard stoop and stairway into a more welcoming landing for visitors. These owners used brick and limestone blocks—echoing the architecture—to transform what was once a single-width path into a small courtyard and a walkway that reaches to the driveway.

steps

A mix of different types of flagstone makes a lovely natural statement for this combination stairway, path, and portico.

Large slabs of flagstone, carefully sited and supported with a layer of smaller pieces, make a natural stairway for a woodsy home that sits below street level.

Worked into an interesting geometric pattern, smooth-cut flagstone leads visitors up a sloping property. Plantings and discreet metal lighting tuck the stepped path more comfortably into the environment.

Poured concrete can be cast and molded into decorative stairwells. Leading to a front terrace also made of concrete, this one is well-lit for safety.

To create a larger stoop, these owners bumped out the steps from the house and added a raised flower bed. Concrete steps that are tinted and molded to look like natural stone join the natural-stone foundation.

accessibility

Making your home accessible to those in wheelchairs or with limited mobility is important if a family member or frequent visitor to your home has trouble negotiating steps. Every state has useful guidelines for slope ratios, threshold or railing heights, landings, ramp widths, and other important guidelines. You can also find out more about universal design at http://www.ncsu.edu or by contacting the Center for Universal Design at North Carolina State University.

One of the guiding principles of universal design, which is based upon designing spaces that are inviting and inclusive for all people, is that it be unobtrusive so that it blends with the setting. This has implications in landscape design, where creating a beautiful and safe environment go hand in hand. Seek out materials and ideas that blend with your architecture and setting.

Wood is the most common material for building ramps. It's affordable, versatile, and relatively easy to build with. A poured concrete ramp faced with a wall of brick or stone would be a seamless look for homes with brick or stone foundations. To blend a ramp to your house and setting, landscape it much as you would a small porch or stoop, planting up to its edge. A mix of evergreen and deciduous plants along the foundation will screen the ramp. And don't forget how much a bit of fragrance improves the journey.

Porticos add thoughtful architecture and accommodation to a house and landscape. A ranch-style home becomes a unique, modern farmhouse with the help of a smooth asphalt drive, bluestone path, and simple portico.

Wood is the least expensive, most versatile material for a ramp. By designing this one perpendicular to the house and side by side, the owners were able to keep it short and subtle.

ABOVE For a more accessible entrance, grade pathways to be level to the drive and the door threshold. A portico and the path's extra width add to the convenience quotient.

Designing a curved drive that arcs to the front entry creates convenience for all. Made of set pea gravel and edged in stone, this one is graded so that only a few inches separate it from a covered porch.

An L-shape house and garage can make way for an extra wide driveway. A level expanse of brick underscores the natural beauty of this tawny shingled home and offers a smooth surface for parking, playing, or partying.

driveways and parking

● ● ● DRIVEWAYS DEMAND CAREFUL CONSIDERATION in a front landscaping plan. Given the amount of surface they require, it makes good sense to consider how a drive will blend into your overall plan. Given the amount of cash a new or redone driveway costs, it makes even more sense to choose one that's right for you, your property, and your climate.

Though its purpose is primarily utilitarian, a new driveway should be designed to complement your home, landscape, and neighborhood. A new development might require you to install a particular type of drive for uniform appearance. But if you have free rein to design a driveway, there are more options than ever to create one that looks great and lasts a long time.

The size and shape of a lot, its grade, the location of the house and garage entrances, extra parking needs, and your climate all impact the design of a driveway. Also consider that cars are bigger now. Most new driveways are 11 to 12 feet wide per each driveway stall. Older drives were typically designed to be 8 to 9 feet wide. If you or your guests end up getting out of a car and landing on the lawn, it may be time to rethink your drive. Or, as many clever homeowners are discovering, you can widen an older drive or improve its appearance by edging the existing path with stone, brick, or pavers.

Use different materials to signal different activities in driveway/parking combinations. This asphalt-surfaced parking pad can be accessed from the street, but the pavers guide the way to the house and garage.

DRIVEWAY CONSIDERATIONS

before you think about installing a new driveway, consider these things:

THE STREET

Is it safe to back out your drive? Does a busy street or a limited view make it safer to drive forward into the traffic?

EASE OF ACCESS

Can you open car doors and get in and out of the car comfortably, even with things in your arms? Is a grade change too steep or a curve too tight? Can you see to back up? Can safety and delivery vehicles access your home?

PARKING

How many cars does your drive need to handle? Do you need more parking? If needed, where can you make way for extra parking?

DRAINAGE

Where will the runoff from your driveway go?

FUNCTION

Will you use your driveway for more than pulling in and out or parking? Does it double as a pathway for visitors parked on the street? Do children play there? Does it need to double as an entertainment zone in a small lot? Would a smooth, natural, or decorative surface detract from these activities?

AESTHETICS

Would you like to downplay your driveway or break it up visually? Are there certain areas of the driveway you want to accent (a turnaround, for instance) or screen from view?

Update the carport concept to add convenience and architectural flair to your home. This oval, tar and gravel (macadam) driveway leads into—and out of—a covered parking area that looks as pretty as a porch, thanks to its cobblestone pavers and post-and-beam construction.

For a finished look, integrate your driveway into your landscape by repeating colors or materials of your architecture. These owners repeated the mottled red of their clay tile roof with brick pavers.

• designing a driveway

Installing a driveway is an expensive project, no matter which way you look at it. It requires engineering, labor, and dollars. That's why most homeowners leave the project to professionals. But that doesn't mean you can't be involved in the design process. Knowing your options will help you discuss the design more fully with your landscape designer or contractor.

Logically, a straight passage with plenty of space from walls, steep slopes, and plantings is the easiest to install...and maneuver. A straight drive can still impose backing up difficulties, especially on a busy road or with limited visibility. Flaring the drive at the end makes it easier to back up and turn. When space allows, a turnaround slot can solve the problem and give you an extra parking spot.

These simple driveways can present an aesthetic problem. They steer visitors directly to your garage, both physically and visually, distracting them from your home and landscape. Patterned driveways constructed of stamped poured concrete, pavers, brick, or stone can add a decorative touch to the drive to slow the eye down and guide it to plantings and pathways. Another option is to call attention to the garage instead of the driveway by installing vines, a pergola, or a more architecturally detailed garage door. If you haven't shopped for garage doors in a while, you'll be surprised at all of the style choices, from cottage to modern. It's easier to find one designed specifically for a certain house style.

RIGHT Asphalt is a hardwearing material that typically lasts 20 to 30 years with regular resurfacing or sealing. Though it can be mixed with stone for texture and color, this drive is rolled smooth in keeping with the home's modern simplicity.

ABOVE Frame a field of attractive brick or pavers with poured concrete to save money and gain design interest. This mix of materials enhances the stature of this traditional home, whereas a solid concrete drive would appear nondescript.

Add a band of pavers or brick at the street entry to break up a sea of gray asphalt or concrete. This section of pavers also clearly signals visitors where to turn in.

•curved drives and turnarounds

If you have the space, add a curving drive, which provides drama to a front landscape and emphasizes the front entry and house instead of the garage. This type of drive can also ease the problem of the too-steep lot by lengthening and leveling the grade of the driveway. When you have an opportunity to add a curving drive, plan carefully to create the best approach to the house and views along the way. Think about where you might add landscape elements.

If you have a relatively level front yard with a depth of at least 30 feet and a width of at least 70 feet, you might be able to tuck a half-circle drive into your property. This gracefully arcing design clears the way to pull forward into the street and allows the drive to meet up conveniently with the front entry. Since half-circles can link up with straight driveways, adding this element is a good way to update a drive.

Front yards that are more than 90 feet deep offer the option of driveway that goes full circle. Circle or looped driveways often look more at home in front of traditional architecture or on extra large properties, where there is plenty of room to balance the hardscaping with plantings and other landscape elements.

Corner lots are well suited for half-circle driveways. This pea-gravel driveway is edged in pavers, which keep the gravel out of the grass and provide a walkway for guests.

ABOVE When space allows, a circle drive offers many advantages. This brick circle drive delivers guests right to the door and offers extra parking in the process.

LEFT A curved drive makes a more graceful entrance than a straight one. Paved with mortared flagstone and edged with blooming plants, this drive extends a charming welcome.

materials for driveways

Although there are many options for paving your driveway, all come with a hefty price tag, so it pays to consider how each will hold up in your specific situation. The least expensive choice is gravel. The most compactible, hard-wearing type is manmade, called processed gravel. Relatively new on the scene is recycled gravel; sometimes called RAP, it consists of tar, gravel, and crushed stone. It's less expensive than gravel and lasts longer, but it has a dark, muddy finish rather than the white of processed gravel. If money is an issue, either makes a solid base for other paving options, so you can finish your drive in stages.

Another option is asphalt, which is made of oil. This material has more elasticity than concrete and can be a better choice in cold weather climates where concrete can crack in extreme weather shifts. A variation of asphalt, macadam driveways are crushed stone or gravel driveways that are sprayed and set with hot oil. This system is popular because of its reasonable cost and, depending on the stone you choose, color choices. Both oil-based options can last over a decade with the right maintenance.

Poured concrete is the most commonly used driveway, thanks to its durability. Proper installation will help control the cracking. Its dull gray appearance can be tinted, stamped, or dressed up with stone aggregates.

The most expensive materials are those that have to be pieced together, including cobblestone, brick, and pavers. For the luxury price tag, you gain myriad design and color options. You also gain a driveway that will virtually last a lifetime. In fact, pavers often come with a warranty.

To give your driveway more flair without busting the budget, consider combining an asphalt or concrete drive with a design of pavers, brick, or stone.

Concrete can be tinted and scored to take on the appearance of pavers or stone. Scoring concrete requires less labor than piecing a driveway from individual stones—requiring less cash from you.

FAR LEFT The nostalgic beauty of recycled brick is hard to beat. Matted with an alternate brick pattern and edged in stone, this herringbone driveway puts a classic finish on this lushly landscaped historic home.

LEFT Look for open-cell pavers, or pavers set loosely, for a natural look that blends with its environment. Moss or another ground covering can be established in the recessed areas for an even greener look.

Tried-and-true asphalt is one of the least expensive paving options when you have a lot of space to cover. A low retaining wall defines an extra parking area and leads the eye to the beautiful stone two-story house.

Textured and etched poured concrete takes on a modern flair when scored into large square "tiles." The clean and simple cement edging, metal railing, and containers play to this home's personality.

The best gravel for driving surfaces consists of crushed stone aggregate. The stone is mixed with sand, silt, and clay, forming a binder. Edged to a fine line, a well-kept gravel drive looks as charming as it sounds.

ABOVE Leave an old-fashioned grass median in a tidy stone or cement drive for updated charm. Reminiscent of a carriage path, this two-tread approach acts like a drive or a couple of pathways.

Pavers mimic common flagstones, such as bluestone or limestone, to lift the aesthetic appeal of the driveway. This subtle bluestone driveway blends with the quiet shades of the desert climate.

parking considerations

● ● ● IF YOU LIVE ON A BUSY STREET WHERE parking isn't an option, or if you simply have too many cars for your driveway creating more parking space is an issue. The simplest solution is to add a parking bay alongside a driveway. It can be placed either parallel or perpendicular to a driveway, or it can be angled for several cars. Placed near a garage, an extra parking slot can double as a turnaround space.

To integrate extra parking into your landscape, consider using different paving materials than used on your driveway. Pea gravel or pavers will help a parking pad blend into the landscape, especially if you add screening elements (that won't interfere with parking or turning). By surrounding parking areas with plantings or a retaining wall, you can transform them into

Consider where your driveway might splinter off into a satellite parking area. This driveway circles around the front entry, acting as a turnaround, parking spot, and front patio.

Level areas allow you to play with looser arrangements of pavers set in pebbles or gravel, for both driveways and add-on parking areas.

Take advantage of odd niches created between structures to tuck in extra parking. Terraced with a flagstone wall and steps, this space offers a shared parking space for short-term visitors.

Mix materials to signal a shift in a driveway function from drive to parking. Brick pavers mark both the end of the drive and the edge of the asphalt parking pad to tie the elements together visually.

garage doors

If you haven't shopped for garage doors for a while, you'll be pleasantly surprised at the variety. Here are a few examples to get you started.

This newly built detached garage gets a classic finish with shed doors and eye-catching light fixtures.

It looks custom-made, but this standard aluminum garage door is given carriage-house-inspired details.

This custom wood door is an architectural asset with its bowed top edge and transom windows.

Retrofitted windows give these standard steel garage doors a modern punch.

Top your garage doors with a pergola to add an extra layer of character—and provide a place to hang artful outdoor lanterns.

a landscape's softer side

• • •

ONCE YOU'VE CONSIDERED YOUR LIFESTYLE WISHES AND HARDSCAPE framework, it's time to layer on the textures, colors, and forms of nature.

Selecting the softscape elements for your front yard is a lot like furnishing a home. You've got the structure designed and the activity areas designated; now it's time to fill in personality and softness. Landscape designers rely on the basic principles that interior designers do, including color, form, balance, texture, focal point, rhythm, line, and scale. Though the terms might seem a bit foreign and imposing, you experience the concepts every day through art, design, and nature itself. By trusting your eye and learning the basics, you can create a yard that's as pretty as a picture.

Flowers are an obvious choice for adding color to your landscape, but when it comes to texture and form, you'll need to call on trees, shrubs, and grasses to supply interesting branch patterns and foliage. When you consider how large a plant grows and how that fits with the size of your house and other elements in the landscape—without overwhelming it or looking skimpy within it—you're tapping into balance, scale, and proportion. The other terms deal with eye movement. Designers use focal points—

Imagine how stark and uninspiring our world would be without the softening effects of plant life. This bungalow uses a variety of foliage types to make it appear warm, welcoming, and settled in.

such as a great bench, fountain, or flower bed—to guide the eye to key areas in the yard. Repeating elements or the line created by hedges or fences leads the eye on a pleasant journey around the landscape.

The goal is to create a pleasant whole out of all the elements you have at your disposal, just as designers have done to create the most beautiful landscapes and gardens in the world.

landscape themes

● ● ● A GOOD DESIGN IS A POWERFUL THING. It can tell us where to walk, look, and sit; it can even impact our moods. Before deciding the individual plants and where to place them, think about the overall mood of your yard. Strong architecture helps determine this. Is the house a casual cottage? If so, then you might lean toward flouncy, old-fashioned plants that spill and tumble over the landscape. Is your house modern and eco-conscious? Then low-maintenance plant life that is clean-lined and simple in form would be an ideal partner. Traditional homes tend to be more formal, which can be enhanced by tidy, symmetrical plantings. The point is, while you're considering how certain plants look, consider how they feel as well.

ABOVE A loose arrangement of multiple flowers and foliage types can signal a relaxed mood. In this cottage, floribunda roses, swinging willow branches, and climbing vines mix it up in carefree style.

RIGHT Simple modern homes are enhanced by subtle but organized landscapes. By planting this small, sloping yard in waves of the same plants—tall ones in back, medium-size in the middle, and low ground covers in front—this low-maintenance garden will grow in an organized fashion.

ABOVE Traditional homes are often symmetrical. Mirroring landscape elements on either side of the central entryway draws attention to this pleasing balance.

RIGHT Customized to their neighborhoods, ranch homes were built across the country in the postwar housing boom. Since this updated brick house hails from the Midwest, the owners brought out its prairie side with swaying grasses.

foundation plantings

● ● ● IT'S STANDARD PRACTICE TO SKIRT A house with a bed of plant life. Often, a row of evergreens is the only vegetation that graces a front landscape beyond a couple of shade trees. If this is your story, it's time to branch out.

Foundation plantings haven't always been the norm. The practice of planting evergreen shrubs around a house became popular when builders shifted to less expensive concrete block for foundations instead of the more naturally beautiful brick or stone underpinnings. In essence, planting along the foundation evolved as a way to dress up the less attractive part of our homes.

But the right plantings can do so much more than mask a strip of concrete. Foundation plantings can soften the appearance of the whole house, making it look less imposing and more settled into the landscape. Trees, vines, and shrubs break up large expanses of wall or draw the eye to architectural assets. Most important, adding greenery to the scene gives your home a sense of vitality that static architecture just can't conjure up on its own.

FACING PAGE To create a more interesting foundation scheme, start with shrubbery, but don't stop there. Expanding the width of the planting strip allows you to create a more interesting gradient with medium-height flowers and ground covers.

RIGHT Think beyond the ubiquitous row of evergreens to give your house a more colorful personality. Ruffled rows of blooming plants match the relaxed mood of this casual Cape Cod cottage.

BOTTOM LEFT Vary the plant life while still honoring the formality of a traditionally designed house. Low stone walls create a uniform line for this symmetrical home, while brimming but balanced plant life adds color and interest within the lines.

BOTTOM RIGHT Grasses are growing in popularity as foundation plantings. These graceful fountain grasses soften the geometric lines of this brick-and-stone ranch.

• successful foundation plantings

As with all of the elements of a front-yard landscape, taking cues from your home's architecture will help you come up with a successful plan for foundation beds. Consider the lines, scale, and style of your house.

Symmetrical houses benefit from a balanced approach with geometrically arranged and manicured plant life. Highlight the pleasing uniformity with matching foundation plantings on either side of a center entry. Want to loosen its strict symmetry for a more relaxed statement? Then you can vary the plantings on either side of the house, as long as you don't throw the overall scheme off kilter by placing large plant forms on one side and skimpy ones on the other.

A variety of plant life—including shrubs, small trees, flowers, and ground covers—will also create a more interesting approach to your house, as long as you maintain some harmony by repeating shapes and types of plants.

In asymmetrical house styles, the principle of balance still applies. But you might be balancing architectural features on one side of the house, such as a large picture window or a tall chimney, with plants that are similar in scale for the opposite side.

ABOVE Add curving lines to a foundation bed to break up all the straight lines and flat planes of a house. Extending a foundation bed beyond the corners of the house softens the hard edges and makes this house appear larger.

RIGHT Foundation gardens can be designed for exploration as well as beauty. Prairie-style houses are designed to rise up from the ground like a natural outcropping. This stone-and-greenery bed helps it meet that goal.

TIPS FOR A BALANCED DESIGN

Symmetrical balance happens when both sides of a center axis are mirror images. Asymmetrical balance is a little trickier to achieve. It uses plants of different types, sizes, and forms placed so that each side has a similar visual weight and importance. Asymmetrical designs have a more dynamic presence, but they keep the scene's overall harmony intact.

As you balance your planting plan, keep in mind that color and shape affect how the eye reads an object's visual weight. Dark foliage and solid geometric shapes carry more weight than light colors and loose plant forms. Because of how texture holds the eye, coarse plants appear heavier than wispy, smooth ones.

Start with plants that have mass appeal, such as this large and colorful hydrangea. Place smaller plants around it to add color and softness. Put lightweight plants together for more impact. A single feather astilbe lacks heft, but massing the plant creates enough visual weight to balance the hydrangea.

Add visual weight with big leaves. The hostas' large leaves, coupled with the smaller ones of the hydrangea, help this bed hold its own against the other side.

Maintain harmony even without symmetry. A different type of hydrangea unifies and balances the overall bed without being an exact match.

• more designs for success

The right foundation plantings can also highlight the lines and shape of the house. For a long and low ranch house, a clean line of low-growing or well-sheared shrubs planted along the foundations will emphasize its horizontal profile. If that feels like too much uniformity for your taste, break up those same lines with a few well-placed plants with contrasting shapes. For example, emphasize the entry by placing taller plants near the door.

A big, boxy house benefits from large, loosely shaped plants that will soften its hard edges. This is where scale comes in. Tall trees can frame a large house and make it appear less overpowering on the landscape, just as large plantings along its foundation will visually anchor it to the ground. But those same plantings might overwhelm a small cottage. Remember to factor in the size of plants when they reach full growth, so you don't end up ripping out plants that have grown out of proportion to the house.

Formal house styles look right at home nestled into symmetrical foundation plans. Conical evergreens highlight the entrance, while a low hedge underlines rather than conceals the beautiful brickwork.

FACING PAGE TOP Don't limit your design to shrubs and evergreens. Planting a perennial bed that assures continuous blooms works great in warm climates where a lack of a winter foundation cover-up isn't an issue.

RIGHT Sometimes a house needs a bit of uniformity to anchor and calm its appearance. Marked by multiple rooflines and an asymmetrical design, this house benefits from the straight line of a tidy, trimmed hedge. A center path flanked by matching stone posts topped with urns adds more balance.

more about…

ESTABLISHING THE RIGHT GRADE

Covering the base of your house is only one function of the foundation bed. Draining water away from the house keeps your basement dry as well as your plant life healthy. When water settles around the base of the house, you can count on a damp foundation and basement water issues. Excess moisture also hurts plant life by causing root rot that will harm and eventually kill plants.

The soil line should be at least 6 inches below the base of your wall framing to prevent its wicking water from the ground. From there, the soil should slope away from the house at a 5 percent grade for at least 6 feet. The runoff from gutters also needs to be directed well away from the house where it can be absorbed by the soil or can be channeled along a drive or a dry streambed created with gravel or stone.

the beauty of trees

● ● ● FROM A FUNCTIONAL STANDPOINT, TREES shade our homes and ease our need for artificial cooling. They also filter the air, divert rainfall, and buffer our homes against wind and sound. From an aesthetic point of view, trees add statuesque beauty and enough visual heft to balance the boxy nature of our homes. By the estimates of real estate appraisers, trees can also increase the value of our houses from 5 to 15 percent over bald, treeless landscapes.

Of course, your first consideration when selecting a specific tree is how well it will thrive in your area. When picking out trees for your landscape's design, size and shape count. Slow-growing or dwarf trees, such as serviceberry or Japanese maples, will do well in foundation beds but may get lost in a large, featureless lawn.

On the other hand, a large deciduous tree can counter the scale of the house itself, balancing the overall picture of your front landscape. A tree's branching habits should also influence the choice. A tree with an open habit—oaks or magnolias, for instance—will filter and soften the view of your house without obliterating it. Dense trees—conifers or large-leafed maples—are better placed off to the side where they frame the house rather than hide it. Factor in root spread so that you give roots plenty of room to do their thing without lifting sidewalks or foundations.

A house just looks cozier under a canopy of trees. This established tree was linked to the landscape with smaller trees as well as plantings under the tree.

BELOW Unique and sculptural, trees can't help but add character to a front yard. This silvery olive tree adds interest and anchors a bed of mixed plantings.

FACING PAGE Airy, single-trunk trees add shade and beauty without blocking the view of the house. Here, an open tree is balanced by the round, densely growing tree nearby.

shrubs

● ● ● SHRUBS OFFER AN ENDLESS VARIETY OF shapes, textures, sizes, and colors. There are flowering shrubs that rival the blooming beauty of annuals and perennials. Both deciduous and evergreen shrubs can be planted, sheered, and pruned into a geometry of shapes, including cones, spheres, or rectangles. Smaller than trees but showier than a single blooming plant, shrubs make up that happy middle range in the plant world. These versatile supporting players can fill in awkward areas in a landscape plan, form a bridge between elements in the house and garden, and provide year-round interest.

Evergreens are best at offering year-round structure to the landscape, but deciduous plants help us track and celebrate the seasons. And there are plenty of deciduous shrubs that serve up flowers in the spring, delicate leaves in the summer, colorful leaves in the fall, and berries for winter interest. Shrubs also invite nature to enjoy the sanctuary of your landscape.

Shrubs are versatile, hardworking elements in a front landscape. A mix of evergreen and flowering shrubs adds color and dimension to this stately brick home.

Drought-tolerant shrubs and plants can displace lawn area for a landscape that is easier to maintain and more interesting to look at. Hardy boxwoods, hydrangeas, and hostas mix it up even in the shade of established trees.

Their more compact size makes shrubs ready partners for showy perennials. Sedum, coneflowers, and rudbekia weave among hydrangea and spirea bushes to create lush beds that pop with color.

LOW-MAINTENANCE SHRUBS

these plants are both pretty and practical. Include them in your front-yard plan, then plant them and sit back to watch them perform with little maintenance.

Panicle hydrangea (*Hydrangea paniculata*). Zones 4 to 8. For big blooms even in the heat of summer, plant this lush panicle hydrangea. It peaks at the height of summer with 6- to 15-inch-long, white blooms that cover loose, arching limbs. In the fall, leaves drop but the large, dried blooms remain into winter.

Flowering quince (*Chaenomeles speciosa*). Zones 5 to 8. This plant pops with blossoms in later winter, offering your garden one of the first kisses of spring color. This 'Texas Scarlet' blooms lipstick red. The bare branches turn red or gold in the fall.

Mapleleaf viburnum (*Viburnum acerifolium*). Zones 4 to 8. With this viburnum, the show starts in early summer, when it produces fluffy white flowers. The blooms are followed by red berries, which darken to purple-black. In the fall, the maple-shaped leaves turn from green to brilliant shades of yellow and orange.

Winterberry (*Ilix verticillata*). Zones 5 to 8. The fruit of this plant begins to ripen in late summer, when the leaves are still lush. The berries hold onto the branches through the fall, when the foliage changes color and drops. This plant grows up to 15 feet tall and wide.

Heavenly bamboo (*Nandina domestica*). Zones 6 to 11. This tall, well-behaved shrub sports fall-like foliage all year. Every spring, white sprays of flowers appear on the plant's straight stems, followed by clusters of berries that turn a vibrant red in winter.

'Anthony Waterer' spirea (*Spiraea japonica* 'Anthony Waterer'). Zones 4 to 9. This cultivar is attractive when planted en masse, and it shines as part of a border garden or hedge. New growth is bronze to red but matures to green. Pink blooms cover the shrub from late spring to early summer, but it can be coaxed to bloom again if the blooms are removed before they turn brown.

Chaste tree (*Vitex agnus-castus*). Zones 6 to 9. This heirloom shrub is loved for its nature-attracting fragrance and showy, cone-shaped blooms. It looks similar to a butterfly bush, but the blooms reach up to 18 inches long.

American beautyberry (*Callicarpa americana*). Zones 5 to 9. This North American native has some of the most attractive berries in the shrub world. The small berries are attached in dramatic clusters up and down the stems. The fruit turns a jewel-tone purple and persists until fall unless the birds get to it first.

Glossy abelia (*Abelia grandiflora*). Zones 6 to 9. This old-fashioned favorite consistently produces an abundance of small, fragrant, pale pink blooms that attract butterflies and hummingbirds from spring until frost. It has a free form but is well behaved and semievergreen. Newer hybrids are more compact than the original, which can reach up to 12 feet tall.

Winter jasmine (*Jasminum nudiflorum*). Zones 6 to 9. If you crave cheerful warmth in the cold of winter, then plant winter jasmine. Yellow blooms cover long, leafless stems from midwinter to early spring. Attractive foliage fills in on the graceful, arching stems when the flowers fade.

accessorizing the landscape

●●● THINK OF ACCESSORIES AS THE JEWELRY of the landscape…the final layer of eye-catching elements that add personality and surprise to an otherwise ordinary ensemble. Accent your garden with anything from simple urns to intricate statuary or from fountains to furniture. What's most important is that the object is a reflection of you; if it speaks of your interests and brings you joy, then it's doing its job.

Accessories can be placed out in the open to add focal-point interest to a garden that lacks a strong visual element. Or, just as interesting, they can be tucked into greenery to add a bit of intrigue to your yard. Just remember that you can have too much of a good thing when it comes to accessories. These elements should accent the landscape, not take it over. The most effective accessories—like the most beguiling jewelry—shouldn't be the first thing you see.

ABOVE Small stone plaques and benches can add structure and purpose to your yard. Made of poured concrete, the stone plaque serves as a backdrop for small succulents and a place to mount the address.

RIGHT The stone bench adds privacy to a courtyard as well as a place to sit.

ABOVE Accessories can be as common as a garden bench or as unique as a work of garden art. An artful paving stone announces the beginning of this path through a front-yard strawberry patch, while a carved bench leads the eye to the fence and house beyond.

LEFT Think of a mailbox as a functioning accessory in your front landscape. Dressed with pretty typography and surrounded by lush plantings, this mailbox becomes an artful accent.

ABOVE Natural elements can also be used to highlight plant life. Positioned along a front path, natural boulders mix it up with a low iron fence and a stone cut into a square.

• water features

Why limit the pleasures of your front yard to sights and smells? A water feature adds another dimension to your front yard—sound. A fountain can gush, spray, flow, or trickle, but for many there is no more relaxing sound than moving water. This can be a real bonus if you're trying to buffer traffic or neighborhood noise.

Visually, a water feature can redirect the eye, add a contrasting shape, or even mask unsightly elements. There are many fountain types to choose from: some are fed from an attached pool of water, others can be mounted on an exterior wall, and still others are freestanding objects that circulate the water within itself. There is also a variety of styles available, from earthy and natural to classic and elegant to sleek and modern.

Water features can be designed to blend with a setting in a more natural way. Water trickling from a simple wall-mounted spigot into a shallow stone basin is meant to be heard rather than seen.

FACING PAGE BOTTOM A bird-bath becomes more fun when it spouts a miniature fountain. This recirculating fountain also keeps the water fresh and flowing.

LEFT Building a minipond is a doable project for the do-it-yourselfer. Constructed just outside the front entry, this compact manmade waterfall and pond gush a greeting to guests.

BELOW Freestanding fountains, often made from ceramic or faux stone, are called bubblers. Nestled among dwarf grasses, this percolating sphere joins others made from a variety of materials to create a fun surprise.

A UNIQUE
WATER FEATURE

a bubbling fountain made from a decorative pot brings soothing sound and an eye-catching focal point to any landscape. Best of all, this is an easy project that you can complete on a weekend morning.

MATERIALS

Most of these items can be found at a plumbing-supply or home-improvement store. It takes about two hours to complete this project.

> Decorative pot
> Drill
> Masonry drill bit, ½ inch diameter and 1 inch long
> Epoxy putty
> Barb fitting, ¾ inch diameter
> Shovel
> Sand
> Waterproof catch basin
> Level
> Cinder blocks (2 or 3)
> Submersible pump, with a flow-adjustment valve
> Saw or jigsaw
> Heavy-duty plastic grate
> Flexible tubing, 4 feet long
> Hose clamps (2)
> Flexible screen or mesh
> PVC pipe, ¾ inch diameter and cut the same length as the height of the pot
> Black spray paint
> Decorative stone

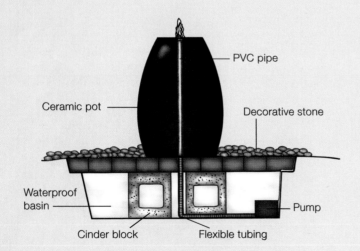

PLUMB THE POT

1. Most pots have drainage holes, but if yours doesn't, use a masonry bit to drill a ½-inch-diameter hole in the center of the bottom of the vessel (photo A). Plug any other drainage holes with epoxy putty.

2. Place the barb fitting into the hole so that the threaded end goes inside the pot. Thread the PVC female adapter onto the end of the barb inside the pot. Apply epoxy putty around the base of the fitting to seal it in place and to make the container watertight (photo B).

INSTALL THE RESERVOIR

1. Dig a hole deep enough to allow your waterproof basin to sit slightly above ground level. Shovel in a 1-inch-deep layer of sand, which allows you to easily adjust the level of the reservoir. Put the basin in the hole and level it. Place two or three cinder blocks in the center of the basin (to give additional support to the pot), and put the pump in a corner of the basin.

Labels on diagram: PVC pipe · Ceramic pot · Decorative stone · Waterproof basin · Cinder block · Flexible tubing · Pump

A

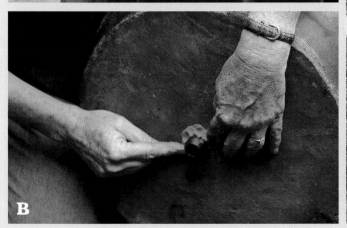

B

C

D

2. Using a reciprocating jigsaw, cut a trapdoor in the corner of the plastic grate that is large enough for the pump to easily pass through. This will give you easy access to the pump for maintenance without having to disassemble the fountain. The pump's electrical cord should be pulled off to the side (photo C).

3. Cut a small hole in the center of the grate for the flexible tubing. Attach one end of the tubing to the pump, clamp it in place, and poke the other end out the hole in the center of the grate.

4. Place the screen or mesh over the grate. Cut a corresponding hole for the flexible tubing, and put the tubing through the hole.

PLACE THE FOUNTAIN

1. Cut a length of PVC pipe so that it is as tall as the pot; spray the top 6 inches with black paint. Slip the PVC pipe (black side up) into the female adapter in the bottom of the pot. Do not glue the PVC pipe in place; you want to be able to easily remove it to drain the pipe.

2. Bring the pot over to the reservoir; depending on its size, this can be a cumbersome step and may require the help of a friend (photo D). Twist the flexible tubing onto the barb sticking out of the bottom of the pot and clamp it in place. Slowly raise the pot into place and level it.

3. Place decorative stones on top of the screening to disguise the reservoir. Fill the reservoir with water, turn on the pump, and enjoy.

front-yard gardens

● ● ●

DRIVE THROUGH THE VARIOUS NEIGHBORHOODS IN YOUR CITY OR town and you'll get a front-seat view of the trends in front-yard landscapes over the decades. What's interesting is how their design differences reflect broader changes in social customs. In the early part of the last century, homes were designed individually on large lots, often with a long sweep of lawn dotted with shrubs and trees reaching up to the house. In the midcentury, house and lawn size shrunk as the population boomed. By the end of last century, housing became more homogenized as families moved to subdivisions in the more spacious suburbs.

Now, the popularity of gardening as a hobby and the desire to boost the personality and curb appeal of our properties have fueled a trend in front-yard gardens. Thoughtfully designed flower beds and garden spaces are winding out from the backyard, where they can be shared with the neighborhood and do a full-circle softening of the house and lot. The garden can be tended while the kids enjoy street-side games that require driveways for bouncing balls and sidewalks for riding bikes. Sometimes called the "two-way" garden, front-yard flowers and mixed beds can be enjoyed from inside the house where they soften the view to the street.

Neatly planted and edged perennial beds bring the grace and softness of nature to the front yard, usurping some of the space more often given over to the lawn. In this suburban home, the lawn is relegated to a lush green strip that serves as the path through a front perennial garden.

picking a
garden style

● ● ● A FRONT GARDEN CAN BE AS SIMPLE AS a circle of annuals around a lamppost or mailbox or as complicated as an elaborate themed garden. Couple mixed plantings with hardscape features, such as fencerows or pathways. Or plan a single floating island bed to balance strong architectural features. Place mixed plantings near the house to buffer the views and the weather. In neighborhoods that lack established trees, a small woodlands grove adds a layer of green and offers a habitat for small wildlife. Or soften the corners of your property with a series or curving beds that together create a garden to explore. But, as with all the elements you'll choose for your new front yard, take your style leads from the biggest feature of all—your home.

Planning a small woodlands garden can give more prominence to small or young trees. With flat boulders and a patchwork of low-growing ground covers, this garden echoes the varied and tranquil topography of a real island, even though it's only anchoring a newly added circle drive.

CREATE A SIMPLE WATER GARDEN

add a fascinating dimension to your front yard with a water garden. No lot is too small to enjoy the meditative, reflective benefit of a pool of still water. In fact, any watertight vessel—from wine keg to ceramic urn to galvanized tub—can become a water garden. Submerge a simple, plug-in pump and add the soothing soundtrack of moving water to your environment.

If you have bigger plans in mind, there are pond kits and decks in all shapes and sizes—though most are about the size of a child's plastic wading pool. Or dig your own from scratch, using felt underlayment and a plastic pond liner. Outline potential shapes and sizes with a hose, but remember that intricate shapes are difficult to line. You'll have to dig down 18 inches if you want to add fish. Hide the top edge of the liner with a rim of rocks and plant life to knit it to your setting. A water feature opens up a whole new world of life for the gardener.

Here are tips for finding the perfect site for your water garden:

• Put a tranquil water garden in a spot where you can view it from your favorite sitting areas, both inside and out.

• Sleuth out a level location that sits high in your yard to avoid drainage problems in heavy rain.

• Most aquatic plants need plenty of natural light so look for a spot that sees direct sunlight most of the day.

• Find a spot that can be easily accessed with pathways and offers enough room to frame the pond with natural elements. Avoid plants or trees that will drop filter-clogging debris into over the pond area.

• Be sure water and electricity outlets are readily available.

• Take advantage of a pond's ability to mirror the beauty around it. Surround it with flowering plants and a mix of foliage. Work in stone and boulders to blend your private reflecting pool into its surroundings and give it even more interesting elements to reflect.

Note: Check with local ordinances and your insurance company on safety requirements. Many dictate that standing water of 18 inches or more must be fenced.

ABOVE The essential elements include a small header pool that will form the top basin of a waterfall. The header pool is where water accumulates after being recirculated by the pump. The waterfall then helps move the water across the main pool to a skimmer box, pump, and hose.

LEFT Surround your water feature with simple plantings so the focus is on the fountain. Yellow tulips offer this fountain a frame of springtime color that picks up the chartreuse of the shrubs.

ABOVE A small rectangular pond creates a dramatic transition in a landscape. This one is sited at the edge of a formal garden, where it marks the shift to a shady woodlands beyond. The pond is lined with concrete steppers and is filled with elephant ears and sweet flag.

LEFT Naturalize a small water feature with a stone border that is level with the surrounding bed. Leave paths through the bed for access to the alluring water.

ABOVE Houses in established neighborhoods are more likely to have lush plantings and gardens that reach to the sidewalk. Here, abundant ferns and shrubbery—all with a mix of growing habits and foliage color—are dotted with perennials and roses for color.

ABOVE The front scape of this urban row house shows how effective small-space gardening can be. This shaded courtyard is spilling over with grasses, hostas, and a mix of shrubs, which soften the structure's façade, clean the air, and buffer street noise.

Small homes benefit from the lush beauty of a front garden. Framing this charming cottage with flowers and foliage keeps the focus on the house while nestling it more fully into its surroundings.

ABOVE In suburban areas where gardens aren't the dominant feature of front yards, keep mixed plantings close to the house. Flower beds filled with fragrant lavenders and roses flank the front path of this new home to soften the views to and from the house.

When you want to create a balance of lawn and garden, a simple plan is to combine mixed beds of foundation plantings with floating islands of color. This center bed keeps the eye focused on the home.

• cottage gardens

Cottage gardens have an exuberance and informality that make them particularly apt at warm greetings—perfect for the front yard! The charming character of a cottage garden is a good match for many American house styles, especially those we imported from England—including the Cotswold, the Tudor, and the Victorian. Bungalows, ranches, and almost any small traditional house can benefit from the bright and natural cheer of this garden style.

To get the look, avoid planting in straight lines or patterns that are too well defined. Mass plants in drifts that weave through each other. Winding paths of such natural materials as mulch, brick, or stone complement the less restrained nature of a cottage garden. Here are a few more elements typical to cottage plans:

- A low fence or stone wall often encloses a cottage garden, becoming a support for plants.

- Fill a cottage garden with old-fashioned flowers that have profuse blooms (peonies, hollyhocks, carefree roses, snapdragons, zinnias, phlox, and foxglove, to name a few) and self-sowing, low-maintenance plants (rudbekia, coneflower, poppies, and columbine, for instance).

- Berries, fruit trees, and herbs can be found living among cottage flowers, reflecting the self-sufficiency of a cottage lifestyle.

Cottage gardens often grow right up to the untamed sections of a property to help blend a house more thoroughly into its environment. This farmhouse has cottage-garden elements all around the house to further that notion.

ABOVE Fences make good garden backdrops. This wooden fence butts against the sidewalk and makes a stopping point for a green garden of low plantings.

LEFT Leave space around plants for more definition and a tidier appearance. These old-fashioned hollyhocks, daisies, and daylilies are planted in rows and separated by mulch to create a tidy look appropriate to the neighborhood.

Exterior walls, fences, and paths made out of natural stone characterize a cottage garden. But they don't necessarily need an abundance of color to charm a yard, as evidenced by these floppy and friendly white roses.

RIGHT The resourceful, mix-and-match nature of a cottage garden goes hand-in-hand with rural life and style. This farmhouse is buffered by a lush garden that includes herbs and fruit trees along with robust native perennials and vines.

BELOW Any small, clapboard house can be considered a cottage. Curving beds and a tumbled mix of shrubs, perennials, and annuals—plus window boxes spilling over with plants—add a big dose of charm to this simple house.

RIGHT Even simple mixed plantings can take on the carefree look of a cottage garden if the design is asymmetrical. This garden takes on a low profile to include other cottage elements into the scheme, such as the rocker and the front porch.

FACING PAGE RIGHT Plant flowers in waves that weave in and out of other species to get the joyful, willy-nilly look of a cottage garden. This garden boasts various shades of red and pink to strike some harmony.

Formal gardens always add a sense of grandeur to a residence, but they don't need to be costly or high maintenance. As this country manor proves, they just need to be carefully planned for balance and structure.

•formal gardens

Unlike the untamed beauty of a cottage garden, a formal garden is designed, planted, and pruned to geometric precision. Often designed with perfect symmetry, using a straight center path that provides an axis for the balanced sides, formal gardens extend the strong architectural lines of a traditional house. In fact, traditional gardens are often planted to mimic squared-off "rooms" in proportion to the house itself, with the plants providing the structure (along with straight-lined hardscape elements). Small-house owners shouldn't shy away from this type of landscape plan; it's well suited to Cape Cods, suburban two-stories, and many symmetrical styles in between.

Formal gardens don't have to be as difficult to maintain as their clipped and contained appearance reflects. Choose plants, such as boxwood or yew shrubs, mums, and shrub roses, that grow in mounds or other well-behaved shapes.

Here are a few more elements typical to a formal garden:

- The garden design is balanced side to side and front to back, often with a center path or point operating as a center axis.

- Masses of the same or similar plantings that all have tidy forms are used. Colors are the same or controlled and harmonious.

- Right-angled geometry is used in flower beds, paths, fences, and hedgerows.

LEFT A formal garden is a well-behaved one. Roses that are trained to climb and boxwoods that are trimmed into a perfect line create a dramatic center bed in this traditional landscape.

ABOVE Stone walls that extend from the house like additional rooms serve as backdrop and support for the simple, elegant plantings of the formal garden. Two matching staircases punctuate the symmetry here.

A center path is a formal garden icon, especially when it's flanked by urns. Though a lawn dominates this landscape, a few elements of classical design mark it as traditional.

• modern gardens

Modern front gardens subscribe to the basic tenet of contemporary design: less is more. And in the garden's case, this means less maintenance, fewer plants, and—in many ways—less worry. A modern garden relies less on plant life than it does on the plain and functional surfaces of the hardscape elements. The goal of a modern garden is a clean and serene aesthetic. It's really a type of formal garden, but with updated shapes and materials. Plant types and colors are limited in number, but bolder in use. Vivid colors and architectural plants add the focus.

Clean-lined, geometric houses, including the simple adobe structures of the Southwest, offer the perfect backdrop for a minimalist landscape. If you feel committed to the low-maintenance ethos, this just might be the garden style for you.

Here are a few more elements common to the modern garden:

- It is marked by clean design lines, with a focus on such hardscaping elements as stone benches, simple wood structures, and natural materials.

- The planting style is bold but simply patterned, with the use of one or two plants that repeat throughout the design to provide the harmony.

- Lighting is an important part of modern landscapes for its ability to dramatically silhouette the pure shapes of a minimalist landscape.

- Architectural plants, such as agaves, grasses, and alums, mark a modern garden.

Clean surfaces and low-profile plantings lend a modern garden its serenity. Geometry plays a big part in this contemporary landscape, which really breaks down into a series of squares and rectangles.

more about...
ZEN GARDENS

Zen garden is a Japanese rock garden. This type of minimalist garden space reaches back to fourteenth century monastic design, and it was created to give visitors a tranquil place in which to contemplate nature. For Buddhists, the garden has spiritual significance and is heavy with symbolism.

Zen gardens include water, which represents the changing nature of life. They also include a dry garden, where white sand—a symbol of purity—is swept into patterns that evoke nature, such as waves. Stones of all types are also important elements in this kind of garden because of the Japanese practice of stone worship. Placing stones in artful and balanced positions allows Buddhists to reference these ancient rituals.

LEFT A limited palette of color and plant life keeps the mood calm in a modern garden. Poured into clean-lined elements and smoothed to a fine texture, concrete is the backbone of this sloping garden.

Most Southwest gardens are modern by default, relying on the architectural forms of the desert succulents and limited plants that grow there. Where a lawn would consume precious resources in this climate, simple native plantings are carefree.

small-space gardens

● ● ● LET'S DISPEL ANY MISCONCEPTIONS YOU have about small-space gardening. First, a small garden doesn't necessarily mean less work. How much pruning, watering, deadheading, or soil amending you do is determined by the maintenance requirements of the individual plants you select. Second, small-space gardening doesn't mean you have to choose miniature plants to get the right proportion. That will just create a cluttered-looking front yard rather than the welcoming garden oasis you dream of.

Plant selection is the key to turning your modest lot into a remarkable place to visit. You can use the colors, textures, and shapes of plantings to give the illusion of more depth and space. For instance, put bright, textural plants in the front of the garden, relegating the paler, finer plants to the back. The lighter plants will recede, tricking your eye into seeing a deeper lot. Sticking to a two- or three-color plant palette creates flow—another design principle that will trick the eye into seeing a grander space. Or, add depth to a tiny lot by creating different levels. Building a raised bed for planting or a small terrace are two options for pumping up the drama on a small stage.

Play to a small yard's ability to be cozy and welcoming by filling it with lush annuals. Nasturtium and lavender soften this picket fence from street side; inside the fence, casual plantings of perennials establish it as a cottage garden.

ABOVE A courtyard garden adds a layer of privacy for houses that sit close to the street. This modern, low-maintenance garden even makes room for a container fountain.

BELOW A small sloping yard often requires terracing, which provides a platform for planting. These large mounding perennials soften the view of the street, buffer noise, and clean the air.

ABOVE Small yards are good candidates for front-yard flower beds. Tucked behind a tall privacy hedge— that also keeps the view of the house from the street tidy and uniform—a perennial garden fills the space with color and texture.

planting an island bed

● ● ● IF A FRONT YARD DOMINATED BY A GARDEN isn't right for your situation, consider planting an island bed. Island beds are freestanding gardens that can be placed almost anywhere in the yard. Connect a floating island to another element in your landscape, such as a light pole, established tree, or mailbox. Or let it be freestanding, centered to your house, or off-center to balance an architectural feature. Design a garden bed to be geometric for a more formal or modern style, or plant a floating plot in graceful curves for a casual, more natural statement.

Unlike foundation plantings, an island bed doesn't have a backdrop. To get the best view of the plants, place the tallest specimens in the center of the bed and gradually scale down to the smallest plants along the outside edge. Include grasses or evergreens to anchor the bed and create year-round interest. If your bed is too large to tend to the center plants easily, add flagstone paths to both separate and define the plants and give you access to all of them. Stone edgings and large rocks within the bed help integrate it into its natural environment. To use an island bed as a screening element, create a berm, or mounded planting bed, to lift the plants a foot or two off ground level. Berms are also a good alternative if you have poor soil because you don't have to dig as deep to amend existing soil.

Use floating beds to balance the overall look of your yard. Two large beds of greenery balance out the house and keep interest going on both sides of the curving drive.

ABOVE Use a floating island to break up a sea of driveway surface. Without this berm, the front yard would lose dimension and the house would not appear as nestled into its setting.

In a front-island bed, foliage can be more reliable than fleeting flowers. Silvery lamb's ear and waving prairie grass offer plenty of interest in this front berm.

gardening to the street

● ● ● THE STRIP BETWEEN THE PUBLIC SIDEWALK and street is a kind of a no-man's-land. Most often quietly given over to grass that is dutifully mowed with the rest of the lawn, this long narrow space can call out to home gardeners as a ready bed that is confined and edged, perfect for planting.

Before you grab your shovel, be aware that this band—given many names, including parkway, median, and parking strip—is part of the city's right-of-way, subject to local ordinances or, in private developments, neighborhood covenants. Often, the guidelines cover safety issues, such as how high your garden grows or how much it can spill onto sidewalks. Common courtesy covers these issues, too. Compact or low-growing plants shouldn't block your neighbors' view when backing out or trip them when out for an evening stroll. Though a parkway garden can add depth and beauty to your yard, if it makes an extreme break from a street's visual uniformity, it can be more of a distraction than a thing of beauty.

This street-side garden also requires the sturdiest plant life to stay looking healthy. Snowplows, street cleaners, and foot traffic can pile on the abuse. For the best results, select hardy, native plants or shrubs. Since this the most public space in your yard, maintenance takes on greater importance.

Textural, mixed-green plantings make for more interesting topography than a buzzed flat lawn. With a low boxwood edge planted as a tidy frame, frilly euphorbia and lavender work with columnar shrubs to screen the street softly.

ABOVE Mixed plantings can be an alternative in areas where even grass has a hard time getting established. Succulents and other hardy natives to this Southwest region are repeated on both sides of the sidewalk to unify the yard.

A fence and flower bed designed within the median can increase the apparent size of a small lot. Trees had already been planted along this street's parkway, so the owners filled in with an open-design fence and a bright mix of annuals and perennials.

container gardens

● ● ● PART ACCESSORY AND PART MINI PLANTING bed, container gardens can pump up a front yard's personality without a huge investment in time, energy, or dollars. Containers don't even ask for much of a commitment—you can move them on a whim and replant them with the seasons. There are containers in countless shapes, colors, and styles letting you complement your architecture and landscape or contrast it for interest. Large containers, or a mass of them, can create a focal point or mark a transition in a landscape.

When designing a container garden, combine plants the same way you would if you were planting them in the ground. If you're combining more than one plant in a large pot, position the tallest plant with an upright growing habit in the center (or slightly off center if you want a less formal look), a few trailing plants along the edges, and some small mounding plants in between. Or mass containers with single plants into a grouping, using similar colors, plants, or container styles to tie the individual pots into a well-designed whole.

Shallow bowls with a generous radius have a simple grace that can work with all home styles. Plants with a habit of spreading and trailing, such as these floppy petunias, are well suited to this container type.

ABOVE Containers are artful accents in their own right. This one has been converted into a bubbler fountain and looks as refreshing as a tall drink of water in this California garden.

LEFT Soften corners and screen unsightly pockets of your yard with well-placed containers. Pick plants that have some height and width to cover the area you're masking.

ABOVE A basic design principle holds that grouping objects in odd numbers—say, three or five—will assure eye appeal for the more difficult asymmetrical arrangement. The lesson succeeds with these three mismatched pots. Using vessels cast of the same colors and materials, plus plants with well-defined leaves, adds even more harmony to the grouping.

CREATIVE CONTAINER GARDEN

Container gardens, despite their compact natures, give you huge opportunity to experiment with design. Within reason, plants can be placed, rethought, and rearranged until you feel good about your creation. Here are some artful ideas to get you started.

Big, bold, leafy plants form the structure of this abundant, 13-plant arrangement (photo a). For full-to-bursting gardens, choose plants that do well in cramped corners. Limit the colors—of both foliage and flowers—to three shades. Primarily in the red family, this garden contains the surprising mix of a banana palm and dahlias. When soil is tight, be sure to fertilize weekly.

When putting together a container, zero in on leaves first (photo b). Flowers are nice, but they come and go. If you can assemble a container combination that looks good with the foliage alone, then flowers are a bonus. When mixing and matching plants, also keep their textures in mind. Choosing a blend of glossy, matte, or fuzzy leaves adds another level of interest, as does combining fine, broad, rounded, or jagged foliage. The star of this container is the variegated begonia, which provides a lot of interest whether it's blooming or not.

Frilly, see-through foliage comes first, so you can plant smaller plants under its canopy (photo c). The airy form of a golden elderberry can inspire countless combinations, especially with plants that echo its yellowish tones. By varying the leaf type dramatically but using similar hues, you'll create a lively arrangement, not a busy one.

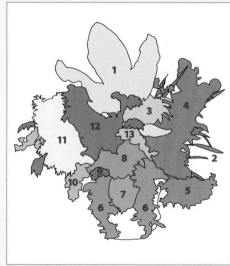

1. Red Abyssinian banana (*Ensete ventricosum* 'Maurelii'). Zones 9 to 11.

2. Purple New Zealand flax (*Phormium tenax* 'Purpureum'). Zones 8 to 11.

3. Casa blanca Oriental lily (*Lilium* 'Casa Blanca'). Zones 6 to 9.

4. Nicky K dahlia (*Dahlia* 'Nicky K'). Zones 8 to 11.

5. Dusty miller (*Senecio vira-vira*). Zones 8 to 10.

6. English ivy (*Hedera helix*). Zones 5 to 11.

7. Blue fescue (*Festuca glauca*). Zones 4 to 8.

8. Red bedding dahlia (*Dahlia*). Zones 8 to 11.

9. Sizzler burgundy salvia (*Salvia splendens* 'Sizzler Burgundy'). Annual.

10. Coral bougainvillea (*Bougainvillea* 'Coral'). Zones 9 to 11.

11. Lion's ear (*Leonotis leonurus*). Zones 10 to 11.

12. Honey bush (*Melianthus major*). Zones 8 to 11.

13. Meteor sedum (*Sedum spectabile* 'Meteor'). Zones 4 to 9.

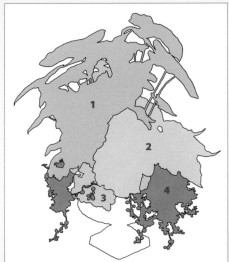

1. Excalibur caladium (*Caladium bicolor* 'Excalibur'). Zones 10 to 11.

2. Fairy rex begonia (*Begonia* 'Fairy'). Zone 11.

3. Mint frost heuchera (*Heuchera* 'Mint Frost'). Zones 4 to 9.

4. Creeping wire vine (*Muehlenbeckia axillaris*). Zones 8 to 10.

1. 'Sutherland Gold' elderberry (*Sambucus racemosa* 'Sutherland Gold'). Zones 3 to 7.

2. 'Caramel' heuchera (*Heuchera* 'Caramel'). Zones 4 to 9.

3. Bowles' golden sedge (*Carex elata* 'Aurea'). Zones 5 to 9.

4. 'Gold Tips' spikemoss (*Selaginella kraussiana* 'Gold Tips'). Zones 6 to 10.

5. Fiber-optic grass (*Isolepis cernua*). Zones 8 to 10.

• window gardens

Window boxes are a two-for-one deal. Mounted under your home's front windows, they are charming architectural accents. And they're also a way to add more garden color—at eye level to boot. Like freestanding containers, window boxes are at their best when they're brimming with vegetation. A mix of upright and trailing plants will have the best effect, whether you're inside looking out or outside looking in.

Choose a window box that echoes the architectural style of your home. To avoid a choppy look, match the color of the box with the color of the window trim so your window and its boxy companion read as one unit.

Repeat colors in your window box and foundation plantings for a quiet, harmonious appearance. Purple hydrangea bushes reach up to these window boxes for a lush look.

LEFT Though window boxes mounted on the shady side of your house will limit your plant choices, they allow you to plant more creatively. Using only foliage plants that offer a mix of leaves and growing habits, these gardeners don't miss flowers.

BELOW Repetition and variety are design elements that will link paired or multiple window boxes. These front boxes were planted to be mirror images, with coleus for height and color, and potato vine for contrast.

the edible garden

●●● DECORATIVE FLOWER GARDENS AND vegetable gardens are often kept separate in the garden... and especially the front-yard garden. But now, creative gardeners have integrated plants that both look nice and offer something to eat.

Not every plant that bears fruit is suitable for the front yard. Many fruit-bearing plants are more prone to insect and disease. Rather than dousing your yard with pesticides, consider plants and fruit trees that are naturally resistant to pests, such as cherry trees and low-growing blueberries and lingonberries.

Vegetables aren't off-limits either. Well-behaved pepper plants and row crops, such as broccoli, are pretty in their own right. Even straight and tall sweet corn plants can add height and privacy to your front plot. For plants that have a more rambling growing habit, such as tomatoes, consider corralling them in container gardens or tying them to trellis or fencing.

FACING PAGE Fill flower beds with a variety of plants and containers to create a lush front-yard oasis. In this no-lawn yard, a variety of mounding plants links visually to round containers filled with vegetable plants.

ABOVE Whether you're in a rural or suburban setting, a patch of sweet corn needn't look out of place in the front yard. This raised-bed garden offers a surprising foreground for this house as well as a bounty of summer vegetables.

Use tomato cages for sculptural interest and to keep vegetable plants in line. Young tomato plants are interplanted with mums for the best of both worlds in this container.

property boundaries

● ○ ○

THERE ARE AS MANY WAYS TO DEFINE THE PERIMETER OF YOUR FRONT yard as there are reasons to do so. Hedges and plantings can screen an unsightly view to the street or add privacy (from both sights and sounds) when neighboring houses in an area are sited closely together. Or maybe you want to define a front courtyard or add dimension to a squared-off lot by creating undulating garden beds. Periphery plantings can also play a protective role by buffering your home against wind and weather, or even defining a place for the children to stay and play.

Still, there are outside factors to consider as you define and decorate your front yard. What you choose will also make a statement about how you want to relate to your neighbors and how you want your house to relate to the neighborhood. Loose plantings, low walls, or open fences are more inviting; dense hedges, high fences, and solid walls can be imposing. Sometimes your choices are limited by local ordinances (especially if you are building a solid wall), but they should also be influenced by the fact that front yards are semipublic spaces and contribute to the overall character of the neighborhood.

In neighborhoods where space is tight, the right periphery plantings can define and add interest to your property. This mix of low-growing greenery, tall hedges, and walls is designed with style and function in mind.

Making a front yard more inviting, while still adding the privacy elements you need, can be as easy as leaving a strip of space between a fence and a sidewalk for a colorful strip of annuals. Or add a gate that offers a glimpse inside. If you live in a conservative neighborhood and seem to be the first one on the block to branch out into front-yard landscaping, start slowly with corner beds planted with a mix of flowers, shrubs, and small trees.

fence lines

●●● WOOD HAS BEEN THE MATERIAL OF CHOICE for fences, mostly because it's affordable and easy to build with. And unlike hedges and plantings, which can take time to fill in, wooden fences have an immediate impact on the environment.

Painted wood requires some maintenance. A fencerow needs a fresh coat of paint every three or four years, depending on how harsh your climate is. Even then wood has a limited lifetime before it naturally breaks down.

Traditional iron fencing comes with a much higher price tag but stands virtually forever with limited upkeep. Like residential design itself, fencing is influenced by the culture and climate of the region. Wrought-iron fencing is a common sight in the South, for instance. Move to the North and Midwest to see picket fences aplenty. Out West, leave it to the Californians to bring modern fencing styles to the front yard, with alternative materials like bamboo and woven metals.

Lattice fencing has a pattern that is both modern and familiar. Reinforced with stone posts, these lattice sections are sturdy enough to support abundant climbing roses.

Wooden, split-rail fencing has an inviting openness even though it offers a strong sense of privacy. In this small yard, a stained split rail is planted for extra privacy and a more natural look. The owner shifted to vertical pickets to define the entry.

Wrought-iron fencing lends a sense of enclosure and stately elegance to traditional houses. This open-style fence is softened by low-growing ivy.

If fences aren't typical in your neighborhood, start slowly when adding fencing or other periphery elements. Placed on either side of the driveway, this compact combination of stone, pickets, and petals still adds a sense of enclosure.

more about...
SYNTHETIC FENCE MATERIALS

fences aren't always made from natural materials. Vinyl, PVC, polypropylene, and even recycled plastics are popping up in residential use. Synthetic fence is available preformed in a wide mix of styles, and many are given a wood-grain texture. Manmade fence posts are often fitted over a preset post of wood, rebar, or pipe to boost their durability. Synthetics offer the promise of low or no maintenance and easy cleaning. But weigh those benefits against a few of the disadvantages: Quality synthetic fences can cost more than wood, and less expensive models don't offer the durability of natural materials. Less expensive synthetic materials and construction, however, aren't as durable as other nonsynthetic options.

g a l l e r y

fence styles

The type of fence you choose can underscore your style or update it. Encircling a ranch house with a modern fence can bring out its clean, contemporary lines. On the other hand, a simple picket fence will bring out a home's modest, cottage-style demeanor. The fence you choose will also determine how much privacy and security you gain. Write down your goals for fencing as you make the final decision about what type is best for you, your family, and your home's façade.

RIGHT With its familiar charm, classic picket fencing will outline your front lot and secure your perimeter, without appearing unfriendly. This two story sits close to the street, but a traditionally styled post-and-picket fence underscores the home's elegance while visually buffering the house.

LEFT Iron fencing topped with discouraging finials offers long-lasting beauty and security. Though hardworking, this white, wrought-iron fence has a delicate appearance, in part thanks to shrubs and trees with an open growing habit.

ABOVE A tall privacy fence will seem less imposing if its design includes cutouts that invite passersby to get a glimpse beyond. Installed along the side of the front yard, this fence screens the view and offers a backdrop for a mixed perennial bed.

ABOVE Be creative with readymade materials to make a personal statement. Without horizontal rails, this tightly spaced series of hollow wrought-iron posts looks like modern art, but it still gets the job done.

BELOW Combine fence elements with stone works for a unique and artful border. A low, poured-concrete wall, studded with posts cut on the diagonal, borders and reinforces the style of a modern house.

One advantage of fencing along the sides of your lot is that a fence makes a 3D version of your property line. When both you and your neighbor are gardeners, fences contain plants to their respective side of the line and offer a more solid backdrop for the plantings.

Limit fence heights to less than 4 feet if you want to be able to interact with neighbors over it. Decorative wood fencing adds a privacy layer without closing off the yard. Cottage-style plantings of carefree roses and zinnias underscore the friendly look.

Custom design a wood fence to meet the specific needs your lot presents. This cedar fence is designed along the curve of a driveway and given staggered heights for maximum privacy. A narrow bed of soft greens works with stone edging to give it woodlands appeal.

•fences and flowers

Made mostly of straight, uniform lines, fence structures can seem a bit rigid. Couple their geometry with a squared-off house and drive, and it all can appear more hard-edged than you'd like. That's why flowers and foliage are pretty softening agents for an upright, uptight fence. You can dress up any fence—and make it seem more a part of its surroundings—with the right plantings.

On the other hand, a fence can do a lot for the plantings as well, keeping them in line and offering support when needed. Even an open fence can offer a straight edge for trimming plants away from the sidewalk and maintaining a tidier-looking perimeter. When pairing up fences and flowers, keep proportion in mind. You don't want tall plants to engulf an attractive fence. Alternatively, a skimpy flower bed can quickly diminish the stature of a tall, elegant fence line.

Painted white for a crisp look, a split-rail fence gets extra charm when joined by a bed of flowers and mixed greens. This corner bed is given structure with evergreens and shrubs and softness with roses, daylilies, and grasses.

Mixing up construction materials is another way to give a front fencerow decorative flair. Stone posts topped with classic lanterns—along with a frilly hedge of white roses—break up the straight lines of these metal fence rails.

stone works

For a more permanent, and in some cases more private, front-yard enclosure, look at options that can be played out in stone. From rugged natural stone to traditional brick to smooth poured concrete, outdoor walls have a strong character. And a lasting one—stone dividers can outlast both homeowner and home! Keep in mind that stone walls over 3 feet high will need to be mortared, while one that comes in under the 3-foot mark can be dry stacked.

The high cost of the materials and the skilled labor needed to do most masonry projects make this choice more expensive than fences and plantings. To get the rich look of stone at a more affordable price point, consider mixing stone works with fencing or even a hedge with a dense growing habit.

Brick has a classic look that blends with most house styles. A grid of cutouts makes this brick wall more interesting and inviting.

Use stone in conjunction with sections of fence and hedge for a stately presence. By repeating the same material used in the foundation, the designer's brick posts tie the home's façade into the landscape.

Combining brick with wood is one way to lower costs—and raise the heights—of masonry projects. Greenery planted against the brick will make it look less austere. In this case, vines climb up and over the pickets for further softening.

Even low stone walls can give a standard front yard the romantic feel of a garden room. Here, corner trees and "walls" of blooming greenery furthers that feeling.

A gate adds security and a sense of grandeur to an enclosed front yard. White-painted fencing and a gate make this stone wall more open and inviting.

gates and arbors

● ● ● IF A WALL OR A FENCE SUITS YOUR FANCY, you'll need to figure out how to create an exterior entry point for visitors. Make it visible so your guests don't need to figure a way into your world; make it eye-catching and you've added another intriguing element to your front landscape. A simple break in the fence line will signal the entry point, but a gate adds a nice finishing touch.

Gates work just as well with fences as they do with walls. Though fence gates typically match extensions of the fence, they don't have to. Take a cue from wall designs, where the gate has to be created out of an alternate but complementary material. Heavy-duty—and heavily detailed— wooden gates blend with just about any type of masonry walls. Iron gates also have the right stuff to join with stone, if they aren't too delicate in design. For a thoughtful welcoming touch, add a light source to your gated entry, especially if your enclosure blocks light from the house.

A simple wooden gate can accent almost any type of enclosure. This bowed design is painted to match the house, but the blue is a pretty complement to an arborvitae hedge.

Though a gate obviously adds security to a fence or wall, it can also enhance the overall design. This tall picket gate breaks up the uniformity—without disturbing the rhythm—of this crisp wood and bluestone pairing.

Decorative gates punctuate a front landscape. In this case, the friendly lattice and arbor construction rises to a focal point and extends a beguiling invitation that would be tough to resist.

gates

Gates that span the width of the garden need to work harder not to be too imposing. Borrowing the friendly lattice design from the fence, the insets in this electric wooden gate offer an invitation to glimpse inside.

Iron and stone are both from the earth, making them good companion materials. This ornate wrought-iron example hints at the owner's love of gardening, as do the carefully tended beds and container gardens. Even the well-planted lighting plays along.

RIGHT Low garden fences define and buffer a property, without obscuring the view to and from the neighborhood. This simple arched gate breaks the monotony, but not the rhythm, of the undulating picket fence.

BELOW A shift in color or materials and a sense of fun can charm an entry. With a pergola that mimics the cottage style of the home and landscape, this gated entry bids a charming greeting.

• arbors

Entryway arbors direct visitors to their destination with style and a touch of romance. Garden arbors can't help but extend a friendly welcome; this type of arched pass-through is designed for walking under. Icons in cottage and traditional gardens, arbors can be casual or formal in style. No matter if they're placed at an entrance to a front garden or somewhere down the path, an arbor's function is to emphasize an area of the garden and add a point of interest.

Arbors don't need to match a fence, but they should have a similar visual weight. Matching some elements—a design motif or the color, for instance—will strengthen the visual link between the overarching arbor and the fence it connects. When an arbor is coupled with a wall or a hedge, the arbor should be constructed from timbers at least 4 inches thick to maintain the visual balance.

TOP Deep arches can accommodate built-in or freestanding benches for a little added romance. Both extra wide and extra deep, this arbor design stands in for a front porch.

RIGHT Place an arbor inside a front gate to create a vestibule that furthers the notion of this as your outdoor entryway. Rising up to a graceful gothic arch, this entry even includes a hanging pendant light.

THE BEST VINES
FOR ARBORS

@n arbor is a small area for a vine to grow, so you'll want to shop for climbing plants that are more delicate by nature. Fast-growing or invasive vines require meticulous pruning to prevent their overwhelming an entry arbor and eventually harming the structure.

Here are some good choices:

- Clematis
- Honeysuckle
- Sweet pea
- Climbing nasturtium
- Roses
- Variegated kiwi

Vines to be cautious of:

- Trumpet vine
- Wisteria
- English ivy
- Some grape varieties

ABOVE For do-it-yourself satisfaction, look for arbors sold as kits at home-improvement stores. Many are made of pressure-treated wood for carefree durability.

RIGHT Even a section of wrought iron or tubular steel can be bent into an arch that signals an entry. A vintage hanging lantern is as pretty by day as it is practical at night.

hedges

● ● ● PLANTING A HEDGEROW IS LESS EXPENSIVE than most fences and walls, but it requires more patience and maintenance. If you're willing to wait a few years for a hedge to fill in, you'll be rewarded with a soft wall of greenery. When local codes or neighborhood covenants prevent building a fence or wall, a hedge can be an acceptable alternative.

Hedges offer more versatility than is apparent at first glance. You can prune a hedge to be 12 inches tall…or 12 feet. Depending on a shrub's growth habit or how dramatically you vary types of shrubs in a mixed hedge, you can create an informal or a formal enclosure for your yard. Best of all, you can select shrubs that add walls of texture, color, and fragrance.

Like most other garden elements, a hedge type should complement the style and mood of your architecture. A row of boxwoods trimmed with precision complement the formal symmetry of a center-hall colonial house, for instance, while a mixed lineup of flowers and shrubs left to their own growing patterns underscores the casual nature of a cottage home.

To keep a hedge looking healthy from top to bottom, taper it at the top. Keeping it narrower at the top allows all branches to be exposed to sunlight. Coupling a low fence with a hedgerow can mask bottom branches and add interesting layers.

ABOVE An informal, hydrangea hedge underscores the nostalgic charm of this cottage. Mixing in tall grasses and other flowering shrubs adds both interest and softness.

LEFT Plants that respond best to clipping are the best choices for formal or modern hedges. Evergreens and small-leaved deciduous plants respond well to shearing.

A tidy hedge makes a naturally contrasting backdrop for medium-size annuals and perennials. With soft purple as a common color, this mixed-flower border exudes a subtle grace.

•mixed plantings

Border beds composed of flowers, shrubs, and trees are another option for creating a nature-based enclosure for your yard. Usually planted in curving or undulating beds rather than in straight rows, mixed periphery plantings have a looser, more natural feel to them. Use mixed plantings to soften a formal house or complement a casual one. One benefit of mixed plantings is their nonuniformity. You can more easily screen unwanted views while you preserve and frame desirable ones.

Mixed plantings can be low or high or composed of a mix of both. They can be dense or open and loose, depending on whether you want to screen for privacy or simply to mark your periphery. If you want to include trees or large shrubs in your border, you'll need a bed at least 6 feet wide. As with hedges and other growing matter, you should pick plants that won't grow into a wider band than your front yard can give up. Also, select plants with similar growth cultures. If one plant is considerably more aggressive than its neighbor, it will soon squeeze out the more delicate plant.

Tall perennials repeat lines of a wooden fence, making them a harmonious companion. Foxglove, hollyhock, delphinium, phlox, and snapdragons peak at different times to keep the color show going all season.

The elements you choose for a border garden are limited only by your imagination. Layered against the neighbor's hedge, tall burgundy grasses, dwarf palm trees, and gigantic boulders form the structure of this border. Drifts of bright flowers weave along the berm in a vivid patchwork.

ground covers

● ● ●

LAWNS ARE FAR AND AWAY THE MOST POPULAR GROUND COVER FOR residential landscapes…and for good reason. A patch of green grass is ideal for playing games, spreading out a picnic, or even staging a yard sale. Visually, the uniform nature of a lawn links houses on a street. Culturally, a plush lawn is a source of pride.

But a lawn isn't the only option for covering your personal patch of ground. In fact, in areas that don't receive the right mix of sun and rain, lawns are high maintenance. Even where the conditions are right, we spend a lot of time mowing, raking, weeding, fertilizing, and treating lawns to keep them up to snuff.

A better landscaping model would be to establish a lawn where it can be enjoyed and maintained easily and to plant other areas with low-maintenance alternatives suited to the growing conditions. You can pick from low-growing shrubs, creeping foliage, or fragrant flowering covers. Or, your best option might be to pave over trouble spots and create a courtyard or a simple seating area. Maybe mulches of pine needles or bark chips will best fill the bill.

Front yards with a mix of grass and alternative ground covers are more interesting to look at and can save you time and money in the long run. The key is to think of your landscape broken into activity zones. First, note the areas that are too shaded,

Heavily wooded lots aren't ideal for establishing turf. A more natural choice is to plant a mix of shade-loving plants that enhance the woodlands scene.

too dry, or too steep to tend. These are perfect places to consider other types of plant life. Areas that see a lot of action—foot traffic or children's play, for instance—are naturals for an even lawn surface. For quieter activities, such as drinks with friends or reading, there are good lawn-free options.

lawns

● ● ● THE POET WILLIAM WORDSWORTH IS RIGHT; there is "splendor in the grass." Kick off your shoes and walk through a healthy layer of turf, and you'll have to agree. Fine texture coupled with durability make grass ideal for front yards that see a lot of action. A plush, even lawn surface also creates a nice contrast to flower beds or mixed-border plantings.

Most turf grasses prefer full sun, so they aren't the best choices for shady areas. And though most types of grass require regular watering, their roots don't like to stand in water. Low-lying areas that tend to puddle aren't conducive to growing healthy turf. Steep inclines make mowing difficult, and even hazardous, so planting turf on a vertical surface isn't the best idea.

Lawns are the least expensive ground cover to install, but they can be the most expensive to maintain…especially when you factor in your time in doing so. Paved surfaces are just the opposite: They are the most expensive to install but require minimal upkeep. Mulches and other ground covers fall somewhere in between lawns and hard surfaces.

ABOVE Add subtle curves to beds and borders to give more shape to your lawn. Low edgings, such as this ground-level strip of pavers, will keep grass in its place and make mowing easier.

RIGHT For a twist, use strips of grass as walkways between mixed beds. Here, turf is used to define and set off the beds while creating a green carpet for walking.

FACING PAGE The level surface of a lawn sets off curved beds and foundation plantings. Brilliant green in color and conducive to all types of activities, turf is the most common ground cover.

Pick the right type of grass for your climate and your specific growing situation for a healthy lawn. Bluegrasses are a beautiful choice for cool climates.

• picking the right grass

There are many types of grass to choose from, so take time to research their growing habits to decide which one will be best for your situation. Popular grasses in cool climates are bluegrasses and rye grass. For warmer climates, Bermuda and St. Augustine turf work best.

Grasses vary in texture and toughness. For a tidy, uniform lawn, stick to planting one species of turf. Kentucky bluegrass, perennial rye grass, and Bermuda grass are good choices. For high-impact areas, where durability trumps perfection, choose such tough turfs as fescues and St. Augustine. Selecting a drought-tolerant grass can save water resources no matter what climate you live in. Many of the fescues, for instance, have deep roots that seek and tap moisture from the soil more efficiently.

Use grassy areas to set off other elements in your front garden. When the flagstone is set in the ground, it's much easier to maintain your path because the mower blades are less likely to strike the stone.

Turf can be notoriously difficult to get started under trees. Fill in areas around trunks with large stones (avoid placing them on visible roots) and switch to moss or shade grass for uninterrupted green.

more about...
A SUSTAINABLE LAWN

there are many benefits to switching to organic fertilizers. For one, they produce shorter, wider blades of grass for a thicker lawn that requires less mowing. They also reduce the worry of environmental pollution and improve the soil while they feed your turf. Though traditionally organic fertilizers were tougher to spread than their synthetic counterparts, this is no longer the case.

Healthy soil not only supports stronger plant growth, but it's also more porous. Increased water penetration ultimately means decreased watering time. Experts estimate that using organics can eventually reduce water usage by as much as 75 percent.

Organic fertilizers promote the growth of short, strong cells. That leads to strong, thick blades of grass. This increases the surface area, pumps up the photosynthesis process, and leads to stronger root growth. Synthetics produce elongated cells, leading to tall, thin blades that need to be mowed more often.

Ultimately, thicker, stronger turf will make it more difficult for competing weeds to take hold. Insects have a tougher time taking over as well. And with the increased soil porosity, fertilizer runoff is less likely.

Organic fertilizers are more expensive than synthetic types, but in the end, reduced mowing, watering, and treating balance the initial up charge. And you'll have the satisfaction of doing something beneficial for your lawn and your surroundings.

Ground covers spread in a variety of ways, but most often either by sending out roots or runners or by multiplying. Mix low ground covers, such as dianthus and euphorbia, with taller perennials for maximum texture.

alternative ground covers

● ● ● RESIDENTIAL YARDS ARE STILL DOMINATED by grassy lawns, but more and more homeowners are discovering the advantages of alternative ground covers. The biggest advantage is the wide variety in types of ground covers, giving you a range of choice no matter what your growing conditions. And though more expensive to purchase than grass seed or sod, alternative covers are generally easier to maintain. Plus, many ground covers offer colorful blooms or foliage, even fragrance, as a bonus.

Before you decide which ground cover to plant, think about what you need to accomplish. Looking for a fresh blanket of green in shady areas? Need a drought- and heat-tolerant species to take hold in a hot climate? Think about what look you want to achieve as well. You can plant multiple varieties of ground covers for a patchwork of colors and textures. Or establish one type of covering over a large area to create a uniform sea of green that more closely mimics a lawn.

ABOVE Shade-loving ferns, hostas, and sedge are happy in woodland settings. Plant them randomly for a more natural look.

LEFT Creeping cypress and juniper are two examples of evergreens that grow low and wide. Mix them with rocks or other types of creepers for a low-maintenance front yard.

Low-spreading ground covers create a colorful tapestry of foliage and flowers. Here, blue star creeper weaves delicately between other ground covers and naturalized rocks.

•choosing a ground cover

Ground cover have gotten a bad reputation as aggressive troublemakers in the garden. Certainly, some are. The problem is, a few rambunctious species are spoiling the good name of all low-growing plants that spread easily.

In fact, there are some situations where aggressive growers are good. If you have a lot of ground to cover, you will want a species that will grow quickly into a dense covering. Or, if you are trying to stop soil erosion on a steeply sloping lawn, the covering you pick should have a vigorous growth habit and an extensive root system. Aggressive growers include ivy, verbena, Virginia creeper, and sweet woodruff. Often, these hardy growers are kept in check naturally in cooler climates.

NONINVASIVE GROUND COVERS

there are a number of easily contained and slow-growing ground covers that won't run rampant or require constant pruning. Here are a few favorite low-growing perennials to consider.

FOR A CARPET OF SOFT BLUES AND GRAYS: 'Walker's Low' catmint (*Nepeta faassenii*)

Zones: 4 to 8
Size: 15 to 20 inches tall and 18 to 24 inches wide
Light: Full sun to light shade

Compact mounds of gray-green foliage make this an attractive ground cover around shrubs and bushes. The leaves release a minty fragrance when brushed. From late spring to midsummer, they're topped with spikes of purple-blue flowers. A light, midsummer shearing will encourage blooms until fall. Once it's established, this catmint is highly drought tolerant.

FOR CLUMPS OF COLOR: 'Blue Hills' pink (*Dianthus*)

Zones: 2 to 9
Size: 4 to 6 inches tall and 8 to 12 inches wide
Light: Full sun

'Blue Hills' boasts dense blue foliage and pink blooms that, when deadheaded faithfully, will bloom throughout the summer. Massed together, these drought-tolerant plants create a lush area of color. To help them spread, take cuttings after the first flush of flowers and plant in pots with rooting compound; transplant early in the growing season.

Use ground covers on sloping areas to soften the landscape and stop soil erosion. Here, a row of boulders creates a sturdy border for a slope planted with ground covers and native perennials.

FOR AN EASY-CARE CREEPER:
'Biokovo' mountain cranesbill (*Geranium cantabrigiense*)

Zones: 5 to 8
Size: 6 to 12 inches tall and 30 to 36 inches wide
Light: Full sun to partial shade

The best part about the mountain cranesbill is that its perky, pale pink flowers don't have to be deadheaded. From May to July, the buds keep blooming and the runners keep spreading, creating a mat of rhizomes that restrict weed growth. Frilly foliage offers fragrance and texture. To help it spread, dig up underground rhizomes and replant.

FOR INTRIGUING FOLIAGE:
'John Creech' sedum (*Sedum spurium*)

Zones: 4 to 9
Size: 2 inches tall and 8 to 12 inches wide
Light: Full sun to full shade

Evergreen in mild climates, this gentle creeper becomes a dense carpet of rosette-shaped foliage. Bright pin flowers are held in tight clusters above the foliage from mid- to late-summer. Full sun with dry soil is best for producing blooms, but the foliage will be happy in shade and soil that drains poorly as well.

FOR A BLANKET OF BLOOMS:
'Snowflake' candytuft (*Iberis sempervirens*)

Zones: 5 to 9
Size: 10 inches tall and 2 feet wide
Light: Full sun

Showy white blooms will lighten your yard by day and night. To keep the billowy form fresh and full, cut off the top half of the plant at first bloom. Help it spread by pinning down stems to allow them to root.

nonliving ground covers

●●● TECHNICALLY, ANY TIME YOU DISPLACE grass or green and growing ground covers with pavers, poured cement, or any other hard surface, you've created a nonliving ground cover. (Look back over previous sections to review those options.) Other nonliving ground covers are used to fill in blank areas or dress up bald spots where grass won't grow. The two most common types are wood mulches and fine gravels.

In arid parts of the country, extensive use of turf and living ground covers is impractical. Here, finely chipped gravel or pea gravel are common coverings. These options keep the soil cooler and help retain what little water there is. Many drought-tolerant plants such as cacti, succulents, and desert wildflowers grow happily in these mediums, which won't break down in the sun-baked climate. Gravel can be dyed in a neutral hue that blends naturally with the environment.

In other areas, mulches are commonly used. There are many types, from pine needles to wood chips to cocoa hulls. Often, your final choice will be determined by aesthetics and budget. Because mulch is a natural material, it blends easily into a landscape. Mulches also slowly break down, nourishing the soil underneath it. Although that's a benefit, it's also a disadvantage in that mulches will have to be replenished periodically. Mulch makes a good transitional material; it can be used until you have the time or money to put in a more permanent covering.

Pine-needle mulch makes a natural covering for wooded yards. Here, the mulch separates and defines plant shapes while setting off a bluestone walkway and patio.

ABOVE Crushed stone is an affordable do-it-yourself ground-cover option in areas that are hard to grow and hard to mow. A simple footpath of square pavers adds interest and function.

Arrange your mulch or stone into interesting patterns to give it a sense of fun and permanence. Arranged in concentric circles, stone, mulch, and plantings create an easy, inexpensive courtyard.

•creative landscaping

Though the goal of most landscape projects is to remake the wilderness into a neat, thoughtfully designed scene, sometimes it's more effective—and certainly more fun— to mimic the untamed surroundings. This is especially true if you live in an environment that isn't easily designed into submission. Rocky outcrops, bone-dry desert regions, and woodland lots are some examples of landscapes you can recreate in your front yard. Study your surroundings to learn from nature just how to design in a free-flowing style.

Or, go in the opposite direction and turn your front yard into a work of art. Carve out an area for an outdoor sculpture gallery, for instance, or a reflecting pond. Though you still need to consider what works within your neighborhood, your choices are limited only by your imagination.

Join your yard's untamed surroundings with creative plantings. Tall grasses and artful allium create an intriguing meadow in this side yard.

A shallow reflecting pool makes a kind of modern moat for this recently built house. Enlarged with a band of crushed gravel, pool displaces plant life with another natural element—water.

BELOW Mimic your natural surroundings for a landscape that is bound to blend in. A tumble of boulders filled in with scrubby ground cover looks as if it's been there forever, especially when joined by a path made from large sections of flagstone.

brilliant lighting

● ● ●

YOU'VE GOT YOUR PATHS PLANNED AND YOUR PLANTINGS DESIGNED to enhance them. The drive is designed and new trees are beginning to take root. The layering will be lush and welcoming…but you're not done yet. Lighting is the final, thoughtful layer that will illuminate your front yard for function and dramatic effect once the sun goes down.

Sure, lighting elements can be added to a mature landscape, but the ideal time to work them in is when you are installing or reimagining a landscape. Many types of fixtures require trenching or digging; others are best installed in steps and retaining walls. Some of the most decorative and durable fixtures come affixed to stone posts or walls.

The most effective outdoor lighting plans are on the subtle side. And in fact, overlighting the night is one of the mistakes most often made. The goal isn't to light up the whole yard in brash contrast to the night sky; you want to set off areas that will help visitors navigate and to highlight those deserving attention. Remember that planting material, fabrics, water features, and furnishings can also lighten your yard by reflecting natural and neighborhood light. Variegated foliage and bright white blooms reflect evening light, as do light fabrics, glossy water, and pale outdoor seating. Even smooth concrete and pale rocks have a subtle, reflective quality.

Think of outdoor lighting as task lighting, directed at areas you want to illuminate for all who enter. Pale blooms and pea gravel join with concrete landings and light cobblestones to set a path for lighting. Additional light points out steps, transitions in the design, and the entry.

an overall lighting plan

●●● WHEN DECIDING WHERE TO INSTALL lighting, think about areas you want to show off as well as areas you need to point out. Low-voltage fixtures give off enough wattage to effectively light steps and pathways. Lanterns and sconces can guide visitors to entries and drives. Uplights and spotlights set at ground level can wash trees or other plantings with well-aimed beams or accent architectural details on your façade. Plan for multiple sources of light that—when switched on—will add depth, sparkle, and warmth to your front yard.

One benefit of lighting your landscape is to balance interior lighting with the exterior to prevent the "mirror effect" in your windows at night. We've all experienced this: you look out your windows at night and see only your reflection back. Lighting your yard will make the windows transparent again, giving you and your family a less exposed feeling. Landscape lighting should be differentiated from security lighting, where the goal is to set an area ablaze in light.

Use well lights to illuminate established trees, and scones and hanging fixtures to wash a house and entry with warm, welcoming light. Light-colored grasses, rocks, and brick reflect both the natural and artificial light.

SIX LIGHTING TIPS

Attract attention. Uplighting casts light onto an object from the ground. In this instance, the narrow beams of a directional light installed in the ground define a shrub's sculptural quality.

Reflect the night sky. Variegated leaves and white blooms—even pale birch bark or flagstone—pick up the soft glow of moonlight.

Don't overdo it. It doesn't take much light to enjoy the night environment. If you use multiple fixtures, drop the wattage of each one so that the contrast between an item being lit and the surrounding area isn't too stark and artificial looking.

Light candles and luminaries. Candlelight is a warm addition to front-garden lighting. It's inexpensive and portable—hang some from trees or place in hurricane lamps on a front table—and instantly sets a festive mood.

Control the viewer's gaze. As you move around the hardscape elements of the front landscape, set out visual destination points by lighting paths, focal points, and changes in the elevation.

Highlight for effect. Well lights or spotlights that angle straight up are best used on established trees. Watch the wattage, as too much will glare and seem harsh.

Tuck small low-voltage lights or mushroom-type fixtures discreetly into plants to light a path and brighten the flower bed. Well lights also direct warm beams onto swaying grasses and a small tree.

RIGHT AND BELOW Use multiple sources of light to balance areas you need to illuminate. Tiny spotlights on these wispy trees add a layer of drama to this entry, which is also lit by task-oriented sconces and riser lights.

ABOVE Wash exterior walls with light for a welcoming effect and security. Diffuse spotlights by putting a shrub between the bulb and the house.

The best lighting schemes use a variety of low-wattage light sources that put light where you want it without spoiling the twilight feeling of the yard. These fixtures have in common a bronze finish, which ties them together visually.

•illuminating steps and paths

When narrowing down your lighting choices, think safety first. Paths and any changes in elevation should be illuminated. To properly light paths and steps, use a mushroom-type fixture no more than 14 inches high that projects light down without drawing attention to itself. Or, place small spotlights or luminaries in planting beds on either side of the path and aim them horizontally to wash risers, treads, landings, and paths with soft light. For a narrow path, lighting one or alternate sides works well. Paths wider than 4 feet, however, would best be lit on both sides.

To effectively light steps, you can also recess fixtures on risers or in the sidewall of a staircase. Many of these lights have grated covers or hoods that keep the fixtures from blinding users when viewed at eye level.

Landscape lighting is designed to be unobtrusive. After all, it's about the light, not the fixture. Tuck lights discreetly into plantings so you see the warm glow and plantings first.

Fixtures with opaque shades that direct light downward are the best choices for path lighting. This mushroom-style, copper fixture weathers naturally to blend more fully into its garden bed.

Lights installed into stair risers are designed to prevent glare in your visitors' eyes. Look for lights with longwearing LED bulbs for energy efficiency and less maintenance.

more about...
SOLAR VERSUS LOW-VOLTAGE LIGHTING

landscape lighting has gotten easier and less expensive thanks to advances in both LED and solar lighting. LED (or light-emitting diode) lighting offers many advantages over incandescent light sources: It is smaller, more durable, and uses less energy than the older type. LED lights are also shockless and pose less of a threat to children or pets. They are most often fed from a transmitter that plugs into a standard 120-volt grid. The lights are easy to install and are connected by a weather-resistant, insulated wire.

Solar lighting comes as a self-contained unit that uses individual collection panels to absorb energy from the sun and converts it into electrical power that is stored in rechargeable batteries that are much more highly efficient than in years past. Though easier to install and less expensive to run than LED lights, solar lighting is dependent on ample sunlight and can often seem dim by comparison to the LED. Solar lighting is best used where a regular source of electricity is unavailable or difficult to access.

Low-voltage lighting works off a transformer that is plugged into a standard 120-volt electrical plug. Solar lights, such as these, are self-contained units that store energy from the sun's rays in a battery. Both types are easy for a homeowner to install.

• wall sconces

Wall-mounted sconces are the most common outdoor lighting fixtures; they can be both decorative and dutiful. Some types point light upward, others direct it down, but all rely on a wash of light against an exterior surface to increase their effectiveness.

This vintage light is reminiscent of the iron, candlelit exterior sconces used for hundreds of years to point the way to an entry.

The fluted glass on this modern, Arts-and-Crafts-style fixture refracts and softens the light for a pretty and practical effect.

Sconces most often come with translucent shades that soften the glare and mask the bulb inside.

RIGHT When lighting a garage area, use sculptural, oversize fixtures that will add architectural interest as well as ample task lighting.

• lanterns

Decorative exterior fixtures, such as lanterns or post lights, give an exterior sparkle. They are the only exterior fixtures that should be clearly visible, even though they can't do the job by themselves.

RIGHT This simple lantern makes a clean-lined complement to a post created of small bits of flagstone. Its frosted glass allows the volume of the fixture, not just the bulb, to be seen at night.

ABOVE Choose a fixture that complements your home and is in the right proportion to the post it sits on. This classical fixture is large enough to visually balance both the fence and the brick post, and it highlights the house's colonial style.

LEFT Decorative fixtures like this post lantern should create the illusion that they're providing all the exterior light, when in reality they should offer no more than 25 to 40 watts each and be supplemented by additional, unseen fixtures.

FACING PAGE The best lighting schemes combine all the different types of task and accent lights for an even balance of light throughout the landscape. Note how the fence on the right is awash with light, balancing the accent lights that show off the pretty pergola above the garage.

LEFT Accent lighting can call out interesting architectural details. Two lights tucked behind dense evergreens spotlight the decorative gatepost and the niche while silhouetting the greenery.

BELOW Accent lighting isn't as direct and focused as functional lighting. The small, copper can lights nestle into a bed of pretty succulents and reflect off smooth cement to show the way up two brick steps.

• accent lighting

Once safety is taken care of, consider accent lighting. There are four common types:

Uplighting is a dramatic way to silhouette trees or other elements in your landscape that have a sculptural quality. You'll choose from buried fixtures—called well lights—that have a fixed beam and above-ground directional spotlights that can be adjusted. Well lights are best for established trees; directional lighting can wash shrubs, plantings, or fountains with a horizontal beam of light.

Spotlighting highlights statues, a special plant specimen, or other accent that deserves the attention. Be sure to train spotlights away from windows (yours and your neighbors') to

prevent glare. One note of caution: overusing spotlights will look harsh and commercial—the opposite effect you want to achieve.

Silhouetting involves placing a light source behind an opaque feature so its dark shadow is illuminated. This type of lighting is most often used with sculpture or sculptural plants, such as cactus, or thick-leaved trees, such as magnolia.

Vignetting combines a mix of light sources to call attention to a scene you'd like to highlight, such as a porch, courtyard, or seating area. Vignetting and highlighting can create interesting effects, but too much will result in harsh, unnatural lighting.

resources

LANDSCAPE DESIGNERS

Bob Lenc Landscaping
5430 Lower Beaver Road
Des Moines, IA 50310
515/278-2028
www.boblenclandscaping.com

Capital Landscaping
5465 NW 1st Street
Des Moines, IA 50313
515/244-2742
www.capitallawncarelandscaping.com

Dig Landscape Construction
3822 Campus Drive, Suite 219
Newport Beach, CA 92660

Garden Studio Design
3822 Campus Drive, Suite 219
Newport Beach, CA 92660
949/673-5450
www.gardenstudiodesign.com

Loki's Garden
29154 360th Street
Van Meter, IA 50261
515/996-2466
www.lokisgarden.com

ORGANIZATIONS

American Horticultural Society
7931 East Boulevard Drive
Alexandria, VA 22308
703/768-8700
www.ahs.org

American Society of Landscape Architects
202/898-2444
www.asla.org

Association of Professional Landscape Designers
717/238-9780
www.apld.org

Colorado State University Extension
Fort Collins, CO 80523
970/491-6281
www.ext.colostate.edu

Iowa State University Extension
Ames, IA 50011
515/294-3108
www.extension.iastate.edu

Washington State University Extension
www.extension.wsu.edu

PRODUCTS AND PUBLICATIONS

Fine Gardening **Magazine**
www.finegardening.com

Fine Homebuilding **Magazine**
www.finehomebuilding.com

L.L. Bean
800/441-5713
www.llbean.com
(outdoor furniture and supplies)

Monrovia
18331 E. Foothill Boulevard
Azusa, CA 91702
www.monrovia.com
(plant material and information)

Sunbrella
336/221-2211
www.sunbrella.com
(outdoor fabrics, cushions)

VivaTerra
800/233-6011
www.vivaterra.com
(garden accessories and furniture)

White Flower Farm
800/503-9624
www.whiteflowerfarm.com
(plants and accessories)

photo credits

pp. ii-iii: © Brian Vanden Brink; design: Group 3; Builder: Hankin Group

p. ix: © Mark Lohman

p. 2 (left): © Mark Lohman

p. 2 (right): © Brian Vanden Brink; design: McMillan Architects

p. 3: © Mark Lohman

CHAPTER 1

p. 4: © Eric Roth; design: www. anthonycatalfanointeriors.com

p. 6: © Brian Vanden Vrink

p. 7: © Douglas E. Smith

p. 8: © Douglas E. Smith

p. 9 (top): © Mark Lohman; (bottom): © Olson Photographic, Inc.; design: Studio DiBeradino

p. 10 (top): © Douglas E. Smith; (bottom): © Brian Vanden Brink

p. 11: © Brian Vanden Brink; design: Horiuchi & Solien, Landscape Architecture

p. 12: © Eric Roth; design: www. hutkerarchitects.com

p. 13 (top): © Mark Lohman; (bottom): © Lee Anne White; design: The Fockele Garden Company

p. 14: © Eric Roth; design: www. OrrHomesLLB.com

p. 15: © Mark Lohman

p. 16: © Olson Photographic, Inc.; design: Hobbs, Inc.

p. 17: © Eric Roth

p. 18: © Lee Anne White; design: The Fockele Garden Company

p. 19 (top): © Maheleh Azima; design: Richard Anderson, Landscape Architect; 19 (bottom): © Mark Lohman

p. 20: Jennifer Benner, courtesy *Fine Gardening* magazine, © The Taunton Press, Inc.

p. 21 (top): Virginia Small, courtesy *Fine Gardening* magazine, © The Taunton Press, Inc.; (bottom): Steve Silk, courtesy *Fine Gardening* magazine, © The Taunton Press, Inc.; (top): Darryl Beyers, courtesy *Fine Gardening* magazine, © The Taunton Press, Inc.

p. 22 (bottom): © Karyn Millet

p. 23 (top): Holly Lepere, © Grace Design Associates; design: Grace Design Associates; (bottom): © Lee Anne White; design: Paul & Robin Cowley

p. 26: © Eric Roth

p. 27: © Eric Roth; design: www. oakhillarchitects.com

CHAPTER 2

p.28: © Olson Photographic, Inc.; design: Hemingway Construction

p. 30: Holly Lepere, © Grace Design Associates; design: Grace Design Associates

p. 31 (top): © Brian Vanden Brink; (bottom): © Brian Vanden Brink; design: Sally Weston, Architect

p. 32: Photoshot/Red Cover/Deborah Whitlaw-Llewellyn LLC

p. 33 (top left): Photoshot/Red Cover/ Craig Fraser/Habitat; (top right): © Brian Vanden Brink; design: Jeremiah Eck, Architect; (bottom): Photoshot/Red Cover/ Jumping Rocks

p. 34 (top): © Olson Photographic, Inc.; design: Campaign-Kestner Architects; (bottom): © Olson Photographic, Inc.

p. 35 (top): © Eric Roth; design: www. svdesign.com; (bottom): © Brian Vanden Brink; design: Dominic Mercadante, Architect

p. 36 (top): © Eric Roth; design: www. hamlen.net; (center): © Eric Roth; (bottom): © Eric Roth; design: www. shconstruction.com

p. 37 (left): © Randy O'Rourke; (right): © Douglas E. Smith

p. 38: © Douglas E. Smith

p. 39: © Brian Vanden Brink; design: The Green Company

p. 40: Danielle Sherry, courtesy *Fine Gardening* magazine, © The Taunton Press, Inc.

p. 41 (left): © Brian Vanden Brink; design: The Green Company; (right): © Douglas E. Smith

p. 42: © Lee Anne White; design: Jeni Webber

p. 43 (top): © Lee Anne White; design: The Fockele Garden Company; (bottom): © Eric Roth; design: www.oakhillarchitects. com

p. 44 (top): Michelle Gervais, courtesy *Fine Gardening* magazine, © The Taunton Press, Inc.; (bottom): © Eric Roth

p. 45 (top right, center right, and bottom right): Jennifer Benner, courtesy *Fine Gardening* magazine, © The Taunton Press, Inc.; (bottom left): © Douglas E. Smith

p. 46 (top): © Mark Lohman; (bottom): Roger Foley, courtesy *Fine Gardening* magazine, © The Taunton Press, Inc.

p. 47 (left): © Olson Photographic, Inc.; design: Nautilus Architecture; (right): © Mark Lohman

p. 49 (top left): © Eric Roth; design: www. bilowzassociates.com; (bottom left): © Lee Anne White; design: Hillary Curtis & David Thorne, David Thorne Landscape Architects; (bottom right): © Olson Photographic, Inc.; design: Sam Callaway, Architect

p. 50 (left): © Mark Lohman; (right): © Brian Vanden Brink; design: Bernhardt & Priestley Architecture

p. 51 (left): © Mark Lohman; (right): © Brian Vanden Brink; design: Hutker Architects; Horiuchi & Solien Landscape Architects

CHAPTER 3

p. 52: © Douglas E. Smith

p. 54: © Brian Vanden Brink

p. 55 (top left): © Eric Roth; design: www. oakhillarchitects.com; (top right): © Eric Roth; design: www.ldarchitects.com; (bottom): © Brian Vanden Brink

p. 56 (left): © Douglas E. Smith; (right): © Eric Roth

p. 57: © Brian Vanden Brink; design: Polhemus Savery DaSilva Architects Builders

p. 59 (left): © Mark Lohman; (right): © Brian Vanden Brink; design: The Green Company

p. 60 (top left): Photoshot/Red Cover/ Practical Pictures; (top right): © Douglas E. Smith; (bottom): © Mark Lohman

p. 61 (top and bottom): © Mark Lohman

p. 62: © Olson Photographic, Inc.; design: Olson-DeBeradinis

p. 63 (left): © Eric Roth; design: www. shconstruction.com; (top right): © Eric Roth; design: www.OrrHomesLLC.com; (bottom right): © Mark Lohman

p. 64: © Eric Roth; design: www.annbeha. com

p. 65 (top): © Lee Ann White; design: The Fockele Garden Company; (bottom): © Douglas E. Smith

p. 66 (top): © Brian Vanden Brink; design: Centerbrook Architects; (bottom): © Lee Anne White; design: The Fockele Garden Company

p. 67 (left): © Eric Roth; design: www. annbeha.com; (top right): © Eric Roth; design: www.katherinefield.com; (bottom right): © Brian Vanden Brink; design: Hutker Architects; Horiuchi & Solien Landscape Architects

p. 68: © Eric Roth; design: www. hutkerarchitects.com

p. 69 (top): © Eric Roth; design: www. mtruant.com; (bottom left): © Brian Vanden Brink; design: Hans Warner, Architect; (bottom right): © Eric Roth; design: www.baypointbuilderscorp.com

p. 70: © Eric Roth; design: Ned Jalbert Interior Design

p. 71 (top): © Eric Roth; design: www. hamlen.net; (bottom): © Brian Vanden Brink; design: John Morris Architects

p. 72: © Lee Anne White

p. 73 (top left): © Eric Roth; (top right): © Douglas E. Smith; (bottom): © Eric Roth; design: www.ldarchitects.com

p. 74: © Olson Photographic, Inc.; design: Hobbs, Inc.

p. 75 (top): © Eric Roth; (bottom): © Mark Lohman

p. 76: © Mark Lohman

p. 77 (top left): © Eric Roth; design: www. shconstruction.com; (top right): © Eric Roth; (bottom): © Olson Photographic, Inc.; design: Sam Callaway Architect

p. 78 (top): © Eric Roth; design: www. shconstruction.com; (bottom): © Eric Roth; design: www.morseconstructions. com

p. 79 (top): © Brian Vanden Brink; design: Polhemus Savery DaSilva Architects Builders; (bottom): © Mark Lohman

p. 80: © Eric Roth; design: www. bilowzassociates.com

p. 81 (top): © Lee Anne White; design: Luis Llenza Garden Design; (bottom left): © Lee Anne White; landscape installation: The Fockele Garden Company; (bottom right): © Douglas E. Smith

p. 82 (top and bottom): © Douglas E. Smith

p. 83 (left): © Eric Roth; design: www. fbnconstruction.com; (top right and bottom right): © Douglas E. Smith

p. 88: © Lee Anne White; design/build: The Fockele Garden Company

p. 89 (top): © Brian Vanden Brink; design: Horiuchi & Solien, Landscape Architecture; (bottom left): © Brian Vanden Brink; design: Dominic Mercadante, Architect; (bottom right): © Douglas E. Smith

p. 90 (left): © Daniel Milnor; design: Garden Studio Design; (right): © Brian Vanden Brink; design: Group 3; builder: Hankin Group

p. 91: © Mark Turner, courtesy Fine Gardening magazine, © The Taunton Press, Inc.

p. 92 (top): © Lee Anne White; design: Hillary Curtis & David Thorne, David Thorne Landscape Architects; (bottom): © Eric Roth

p. 93: © Daniel Milnor; design: Garden Studio Design

p. 94: © Eric Roth

p. 95 (left): © Brian Vanden Brink; design: Polhemus Savery DaSilva Architects Builders; (right): © Mark Lohman

p. 96 (left and right): © Maheleh Azima

p. 97: Eric Roth

p. 98 (top left): Kerry Ann Moore, courtesy Fine Gardening magazine, © The Taunton Press, Inc.; (top right and bottom center): David Cavagnaro, courtesy Fine Gardening magazine, © The Taunton Press, Inc.; (bottom left): Chip Tynan, Missouri Botanical Garden Plantfinder; (bottom right): Jerry Pavia, courtesy Fine Gardening magazine, © The Taunton Press, Inc.

p. 99 (top left): courtesy Meucci; www. gardensoyvey.com; (top center): Saxon Holt, courtesy Fine Gardening magazine, © The Taunton Press, Inc.; (top right): David Sherry, courtesy Fine Gardening magazine, © The Taunton Press, Inc.; (bottom left): Michelle Gervais, courtesy Fine Gardening magazine, © The Taunton Press, Inc.; (bottom right): courtesy Rhoda Maurer, Scott Arboretum Archives

p. 100 (left and right): © Daniel Milnor; design: Garden Studio Design

p. 101 (top left): © Eric Roth; (bottom left): © Lee Anne White

p. 101 (right): © Douglas E. Smith

p. 102: © Eric Roth; design: www. horstbuchanan.com

p. 103 (top left): © Mark Lohman; (top right): © Maheleh Azima; design: Lush Life Home & Garden; (bottom): © Eric Roth

p. 104: Danielle Sherry, courtesy Fine Gardening magazine, © The Taunton Press, Inc.

p. 105 (all): Danielle Sherry, courtesy Fine Gardening magazine, © The Taunton Press, Inc.

p. 128: Allan Mandell, courtesy *Fine Gardening* magazine, © The Taunton Press, Inc.

p. 129 (left and right): Jennifer Benner, courtesy *Fine Gardening* magazine, © The Taunton Press, Inc.

p. 130: © Brian Vanden Brink; design: McMillan Architects

p. 131 (top and bottom): Steve Aitken, courtesy *Fine Gardening* magazine, © The Taunton Press, Inc.

p. 132: Holly Lepere, © Grace Design Associates; design: Grace Design Associates

p. 133 (top): © Brian Vanden Brink; design: Jack Silverio, Architect; (bottom): Holly Lepere, © Grace Design Associates; design: Grace Design Associates

CHAPTER 6

p. 134: © Daniel Milnor; design: Garden Studio Design

p. 136: © Mark Lohman

p. 137 (top left): © Eric Roth; design: www. heidipribell.com; (top right and bottom): © Mark Lohman

p. 138 (top): © Eric Roth; (bottom): © Mark Lohman

p. 139 (top left): © Mark Lohman

p. 139 (top right): Photoshot/Red Cover/ Simon McBride; (bottom): © Mark Lohman

p. 140 (left): © Mark Lohman

p. 140 (top right): © Eric Roth; design: www.peterphelps.com; (bottom right): © Lee Anne White; design: Jeni Webber

p. 141 (top and bottom): © Mark Lohman

p. 142 (top and bottom): © Mark Lohman

p. 143 (top and bottom): © Mark Lohman

p. 144: © Mark Lohman

p. 145 (top left): © Randy O'Rourke; (top right): © Mark Lohman; (bottom): © Eric Roth; design: www.benjaminnutter.com

p. 146 (top): © Mark Lohman; (bottom): © Lee Anne White; design: David Thorne Landscape Architects

p. 147 (top and bottom): © Mark Lohman

p. 148 (top): © Mark Lohman; (bottom): © Brian Vanden Brink; design: Phi Home Designs

p. 149 (top left): © Mark Lohman; (bottom left): © Randy O'Rourke

p. 149 (right): © Eric Roth

p. 150: © Mark Lohman

p. 151 (top): © Eric Roth; design: www. peterphelps.com; (bottom): © Lee Anne White; design: Luis Llenza Garden Design

p. 152: © Mark Lohman

p. 153 (top and bottom): © Mark Lohman

CHAPTER 7

p. 154: © Lee Anne White; design: The Fockele Garden Company

p. 156: © Eric Roth; design: www. OrrHomesLLC.com

p. 157 (top): © Douglas E. Smith; (bottom): © Eric Roth

p. 158 (top): © Eric Roth; design: www. whitlabrothers.com; (bottom): © Eric Roth

p. 159: © Eric Roth; design: www. markfinlay.com

p. 160: © Lee Anne White; design: The Fockele Garden Company

p. 161 (top left): © Eric Roth; (top right and bottom): © Lee Anne White; design: The Fockele Garden Company

p. 162 (left): Jennifer Benner, courtesy *Fine Gardening* magazine, © The Taunton Press, Inc.; (right): Hilary Nichols, courtesy *Fine Gardening* magazine, © The Taunton Press, Inc.

p. 163 (top): © Eric Roth; (bottom left): Jerry Pavia, courtesy *Fine Gardening* magazine, © The Taunton Press, Inc.; (bottom center): Virginia Small, courtesy *Fine Gardening* magazine, © The Taunton Press, Inc.; (bottom right): Jennifer Benner, courtesy *Fine Gardening* magazine, © The Taunton Press, Inc.

p. 164: © Lee Anne White; design: The Fockele Garden Company

p. 165 (top): © Eric Roth; (bottom): © Eric Roth; design: www.horstbuchanan.com

p. 166: © Eric Roth; design: www.kl-la. com

p. 167 (top): © Olson Photographic, Inc.; design: Vanguard Construction; (bottom): © Eric Roth

CHAPTER 8

p. 168: © Olson Photographic, Inc.; design: Anthony Terry Architects

p. 170: © Mark Lohman

p. 172: © Daniel Milnor; design: Garden Studio Design

p. 173 (top): © Eric Roth; (bottom left and right): © Daniel Milnor; design: Garden Studio Design

p. 174: © Mark Lohman

p. 175: © Lee Anne White; design: Kristina Kessel & David Thorne, David Thorne Landscape Architects

p. 176 (left): © Douglas E. Smith; (right): © Daniel Milnor; design: Garden Studio Design

p. 177: © Mark Lohman

p. 178 (all): © Douglas E. Smith

p. 179 (all): © Mark Lohman

p. 180 (left): © Maheleh Azima; design: Shane Griffin, Landscape Architect of Planters, Inc.; (right): © Daniel Milnor; design: Garden Studio Design

p. 181: © Olson Photographic, Inc.; design: Anthony Terry Architects

also available from The Taunton Press

Editors of *Fine Gardening* magazine
Paperback
$19.95 U.S.

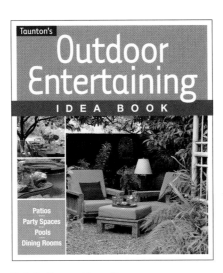

Natalie Ermann Russell
Paperback
$19.95 U.S.

Natalie Ermann Russell
Paperback
$19.95 U.S.

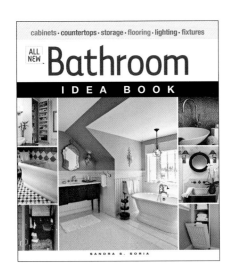

Sandra S. Soria
Paperback
$19.95 U.S.

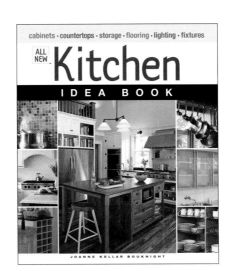

Joanne Kellar Bouknight
Paperback
$19.95 U.S.

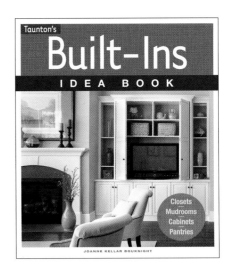

Joanne Kellar Bouknight
Paperback
$19.95 U.S.